EVERGREENS

Other Gardening Books by H. Peter Loewer

Indoor Water Gardener's How-to Handbook
Seeds and Cuttings
Bringing the Outdoors In
Growing and Decorating with Grasses

EVERGREENS

A Guide for
Landscape,
Lawn and Garden

Written and Illustrated by

H. PETER LOEWER

WALKER and COMPANY
NEW YORK

LIBRARY OF CONGRESS CATALOGING IN PUBLICATION DATA

Loewer, H. Peter.
  Evergreens, a guide for landscape, lawn, and garden.

  Bibliography: p.
  Includes index.
  1. Ornamental evergrees.   I. Title.
SB428.L63   1981   635.9'73   80-51852
ISBN 0-8027-0662-2   AACR2

First published in the United States of America in 1981 by the Walker Publishing Company, Inc.

Published simultaneously in Canada by John Wiley & Sons Canada, Limited, Rexdale, Ontario.

ISBN: 0-8027-0662-2

Library of Congress Catalog Card Number: 80-51852

Book Design: Ronald F. Shey

Printed in the United States of America
10 9 8 7 6 5 4 3 2 1

CONTENTS

PREFACE

As I write this preface, autumn is upon the land: leaves turned brown by a summer's lack of water are starting to fall. But they drop without a glimmer of yellow, scarlet, or red, for this is 1980 and one of the dryest summers of recent history. By midafternoon the goldenrods begin to wilt in the warm September sun and the wild asters—also suffering from the drought—merely speck the fields with purple rather than produce their usual vast swatches of color. The skies turn a leaden gray, but no water falls, and the murmur of the wasps as they build nests for the winter blends with the steady, drying winds that blow across the hills.

But walking in the garden, I pass my collections of evergreens. They still glow with color: The needles on the creeping hemlocks shine in the waning light; the arborvitae is still a fresh and vibrant green; and even the waxy leaves of the wild ginger have fought the drought and retain a bit of luster. And all around them the lillies die back and the ornamental grasses turn brown and shrivel, and the back lawn looks exactly like a rather large doormat. The evergreens remain true to their calling.

This book tells some of what I've learned about a special group of plants that retain their leaves for every season of the year and at the same time remain small enough in stature to be well within the grasp of the average gardener and homeowner.

Once again I owe a debt of gratitude to my publisher, Samuel Walker, for the opportunity to do this book; my editor, Richard Winslow, for his friendship and his ability to point my wandering way to the straight and the narrow; my wife, Jean, for her continual support in the garden and additional help in illustrating this book; and finally—once again—the many nurserymen and women who grow the small evergreens, publish the catalogs and lists necessary to build a collection, and have aided me in bringing this book together.

HPL
Cochecton, N.Y., September 1980

INTRODUCTION

They finished putting a new roof on our old farmhouse today. The entire job took a little over a week, and that included tearing off the old layers of asphalt roofing and the original wood shakes and then adding the new layer. As the final truckload of tarry remnants headed down the driveway to the local landfill, I went outside to contemplate our new passport to a leak-free existence and, at the same time, examine the damage to the gardens around me:

Various pieces of shingle that sailed through the air like square frisbees had impaled themselves in the earth in a number of places; old nails pierced the leaves of shrubs and trees like straight pins in a dress pattern; and globs of tar piled up until they melted again to the ground under the late spring sun. The result of the week's roofing activity was that some sedums and sempervivums on the front rock garden bed survived and some did not; most of the saxifrages lost their long spikes of bloom; a number of dwarf iris in one of the target areas were obliterated until next year; and other specimens of rather unique plant life literally bit the dust.

But not all was lost; all my dwarf and small evergreens survived the bombardment. My collection of hemlocks—bent under the weight of old shingles—sprang back like unhooked springs when the debris was removed. Two small Japanese pines planted on the upper slope of the back bank returned to their previous positions when the accumulations of tarry papers and bits of board were picked up. In fact, not one of the dozens of varieties of evergreens was bothered by its workout.

For these plants are tough! In addition to their beauty of form, which enchants the eye for all four seasons, and their seemingly endless variations on the color green—with side trips to blue, yellow, brown, and white—they adapt to almost any condition, braving rigors of weather and insults from modern man that would defeat many lesser members of the plant kingdom.

But not every gardener must face the trauma of installing a new roof, so there must be other, just as compelling reasons for growing small evergreens. And there are:

Some gardeners must—either through choice or misfortune—garden in confined spaces. Any large trees and plants will eventually blot them literally out of house and home. Others must move to new jobs before the garden ever nears completion but would still like some sense of what a mature garden can offer. Still others work in the typical climate of most of the United States, where a lush twelve-month growing season is not to be had. And finally, many people prefer the quiet beauty of a garden devoted to subtle textures and shades of foliage rather than the often garish beauty of many garden perennials.

The popular use of the word *evergreen* refers to two distinct kinds of plants: the pine family, comprising the pines, spruces, hemlocks, and other plant genera with needlelike leaves, which hold their seeds within cones and do not produce true petaled flowers; and other kinds—which are true flowering plants such as the rhododendrons and azaleas, that are generally unrelated by family or genus but share the ability to hold their leaves through all four seasons.

This book deals with samples from both groups.

The word *small* in the title refers to the ultimate size of the plants, bushes, and trees that will be considered. With few exceptions, the plants mentioned rarely reach a height of twelve feet in the gardener's lifetime—or often the tree's. Thus they are always manageable in the landscape and never overwhelm a vista.

In addition to the word *small,* the term *dwarf* is often used in plant descriptions. This usually means a plant or shrub or tree that is three feet high at maturity or smaller. It is an arbitrary designation with absolutely no significance in precise botanical differentiation.

Chapter 1 deals with botanical nomenclature and explains the structure and botany of the true evergreens; the definitions of different shapes; the uses of evergreens in the contemporary landscape and garden; and a few thoughts on the small garden in general.

Chapter 2 covers planting and care instructions, including information about climatic zones and wind chill, soil preparation, sun and wind exposure, winterkill and snow cover, protection from animals and pests, pruning, transplanting, container gardening, propagation, and general care.

Chapter 3 describes the true evergreens, including all the important genera.

Chapter 4 is concerned with the plants belonging to the flower-bearing group that have evergreen leaves, focusing on a selection of those that are more popular and readily available.

Chapter 5 lists reputable nursery sources for plants and points out the ease of shopping by mail. In addition, the various societies devoted to the evergreens and related plants are listed.

The bibliography lists related books on the evergreens that are available in libraries and bookstores.

1.

Definitions

A WORD ON NOMENCLATURE

Although many plants can be recognized by their common, or vernacular, names, there are thousands that cannot—and among those thousands are the majority of the evergreens. A pine tree to one person means any tree that has needles (whether evergreen or not), whereas to another it means one particular kind of evergreen that has needles that occur in groups of five. There must be some system to enable one gardener to tell another exactly what tree he or she wishes to buy or collect or describe, and that system must also allow someone who speaks only English to know exactly what plant a German gardener is talking about. There is such a scientific language of botany, and it is based on Latin.

And this language is a lot easier to use than people generally admit. Gardeners have been batting such words as *Delphinium* or *Fuchsia* about for years never realizing that these are actually correct scientific names. Neither plant has ever acquired a common name or one out of folklore.*

Delphinium is from the Greek word *delphin* and refers to the fanciful notion that the flower buds resemble a dolphin's head. Fuchsia is named to honor the sixteenth-century German botanist Leonard Fuchs. For a fascinating glimpse of the development of scientific nomenclature see L. H. Bailey, *How Plants Get Their Names* (New York: Dover, 1933).

Latin became the language of botany (and zoology) since it was the language of the Church, where most medieval scholarship took place. With the rise of modern science, Latin has remained the universal language of botany, impervious to the changes a living language goes through.

The four classifications of concern to the gardener are *genus, species, variety,* and *cultivar.*

Genus represents a major characteristic held by a particular grouping of plants, much like a family name separates all the Smiths from all the Browns. For example, *Pinus*—Latin for pine—is the genus for cone-bearing evergreen trees with slender needles that occur in groups of two to five along the branches. The term is italicized to set it off from any accompanying text, and it always has an initial capital.

Among the pines are numerous true-breeding variations that lead to the next breakdown, the *species,* also italicized, but without an initial capital. These variations can refer to the plant's size, color, habit of growth, or any identifying characteristic—even its homeland. *Pinus alpina* would hail from the Alps and *Pinus contorta* bears twisted and contorted branches.

The third term is designated the *variety.* This is also italicized and often preceded by the abbreviation: *var.,* set in roman type. *Variety* refers to a variation that arises within a single species that is usually genetically stable and thus breeding true from seed. The dwarf mountain pine is called *Pinus mugo,* but a round and compact form of the tree is known as *Pinus mugo* var. *pumilio.*

The fourth term is cultivar—from *culti*vated *variety*—and refers to a plant that arises in cultivation with a distinguishing characteristic that will pass to succeeding generations when bred by seed or cutting. The International Code of Nomenclature of Cultivated Plants (ICNCP) adopted this term in 1969 and instead of being in Latin, cultivars must be labeled with a modern, or "fancy," name, set in roman type, and set off by single quotes. A form of *Pinus mugo* var. *pumilio* with contorted needles would be called *Pinus mugo* var. *pumilio* 'Contorted.' Older plants that were named before the adoption of the latest ICNCP rules still maintain some Latin cultivar designations, for example, *Pinus parvifolia* 'Brevifolia.'

One more bit on language: in plant breeding, when two

species are crossed in a search for new types, the resultant plant is termed a hybrid. Hybrids do not usually breed true from seed and are therefore propagated, or cloned, by such asexual means as rooted cuttings. Hybrids are signified by naming the parent plants with an ×, or multiplication sign, between the names—for example, *Juniperus × media.*

Nothing in life is sure and the science of nomenclature—though relatively stable—will occasionally change. New rules will be adopted in the future or old rules will be resurrected. And if you get involved in these marvelous plants, as I have, you will begin to search old books and buy plants originally from faraway places. Eventually you will run across all the names and combinations of names I've just covered and, most likely, some that I haven't.

Seed of the yew

A BIT OF BOTANY

The evergreens are plants with leaves that persist over the coming seasons, unlike deciduous trees, which shed their leaves every fall. The largest group of these plants are the conifers, or *gymnosperms,* distinguished from other plants by their needle or scalelike leaves and the cones they bear to carry seeds. The smaller types of the conifers are the general subjects of this book. The flowering plants, or *angiosperms,* have a few evergreen members too, and some of them are covered in Chapter 4.

Pine cone

The conifers, and the vast majority of the flowering plants as well—unlike ferns, mosses, and many of the simpler plants—produce true seeds for reproduction: capsules of many sizes and shapes that carry their own supply of food within their walls and persist with the germ of life for months, years, or sometimes centuries.

While there are at least 250,000 species of flowering plants, with many more still waiting to be discovered and named, there are only about 500 species of conifers. And of these 500, the vast majority belong to the Pinaceae, or Pine, family, which in turn comprises the cedars, junipers, hemlocks, firs, and, of course, the pines themselves. They have resinous and aromatic tissues, usually needlelike leaves, and produce the familiar woody cone. The other family belonging to the conifers are the yews, or Taxaceae; they

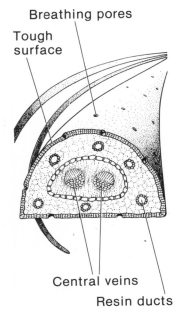

Breathing pores

Tough
surface

Central veins

Resin ducts

Pine needle
in cross section

are different in that their seed is produced in a small cup-shaped receptacle rather than a typical cone.

Unlike the leaves of flowering trees and plants, which are usually thin, broad, and crossed with an efficient network of branching veins, most of the conifers possess needles—from two to five in a group—each one a complete energy factory ready to convert carbon dioxide into simple sugars for the plant's food. Each needle has a central vein to carry water and nutrients to the cells and return the sugars to other parts of the plant.

The surface of each needle is extremely tough and well supplied with ducts to carry the familiar-smelling resins to any injured areas, where the piny liquid quickly dries to form a sealant for added protection. Since there is relatively little surface exposed to the open air, the conifer needle can survive a winter's cold that would quickly destroy a broad, thin leaf.

The life cycle of the conifers is often represented by the white pine (*Pinus strobus*), since more is known about its life history than about any other gymnosperm. The same cycle is followed by all the other members of the conifer group.

Every spring—in mid-June in our area of the country—pollen-bearing structures appear at the ends of most lower branches of a mature white pine tree and represent the male (1). They cluster just below the current season's crop of new needles (2). When the structures are mature, a cloud of yellow dust is released, each particle a tiny winged grain of pollen (3). These pollen grains float with the air currents to the tops of the trees, where the female cones are produced (4). These cones eventually mature into the familiar form that everyone recognizes. The process of producing seed takes two years. In the first spring the pollen grain fertilizes an egg cell in the cone's interior. During the second summer or early fall the cone will point to the ground, open (5), and release winged seeds (6) that will fall gently to the earth, remaining unchanged for the winter. The following spring, under the warm rays of the sun, the seed will germinate and a new baby pine appears (7).

Except for minor variations in the time involved or the type of cone produced—some cones are very fragile while others can last for years—the process just described is the same for all the members of the conifer group.

Our driveway is lined on both sides with a stately parade of fifty-year-old white pine trees—twenty-eight to be exact, with an additional twenty in close proximity to the house and gardens—and when they begin to shed pollen, the air is full and everything is covered: the stones in the driveway are edged with yellow; the tops of all the furniture are coated to such a depth that daily dusting is necessary; sills near open windows have an even deeper layer of the golden powder; and the leaves of other house and garden plants, including all the other conifers in the garden, become a yellowish green from the accumulation of trillions of tiny pollen grains.

Cleaning up the pollen from these trees is a great deal of work, but they, in turn, give their own share of services to us: in winter the trees provide a cover for the driveway and keep snow plowing to a minimum; in the heat of summer they give a filtered shade that is of an airy quality unmatched by that of a leaved tree; we gather their fallen needles for a fine garden mulch; and all winter long the white cold is softened by the green needles of these imposing trees.

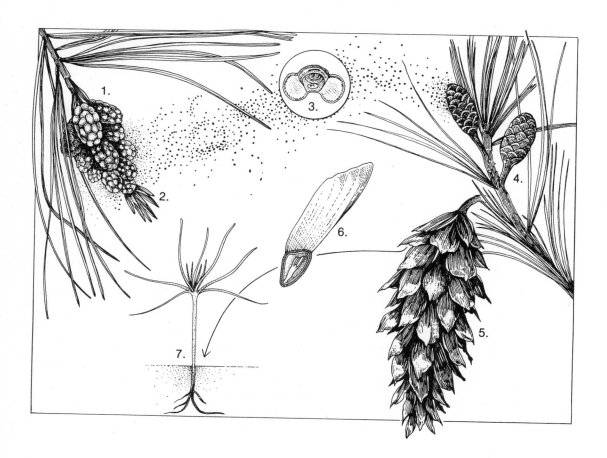

WHAT IS A SMALL EVERGREEN?

The term *small evergreen* refers to plants that are dwarf (three feet high or less upon maturity) or small (under twelve feet high upon maturity, although a few specimens might reach sixteen feet). There are six reasons why a particular plant might be so qualified:

1. It is genetically dwarf or small, and all members of its species are dwarf or small. The Japanese stone pine (*Pinus pumila*) rarely exceeds nine feet in height when mature; paxistima (*Paxistima canbyi),* an evergreen angiosperm, never grows higher than sixteen inches under the best conditions.

2. It grows slowly. A particular species might take two or more human lifetimes to reach its ultimate height. A western red cedar (*Thuja plicata*) might be quite comfortable in a reasonably small backyard for fifty or sixty years, but by 200 years, it could be 200 feet high.

3. A plant might be termed *small* only by its nature of growth. The branches might droop, spread out and sweep the ground, or creep low upon the earth. The tree never reveals an increase in height; instead, its growth is outward.

4. It might be pruned by man, browsed by animals, or clipped as a hedge. By the process of bonsai a normally large plant—such as a fir or cedar—is kept small. Using a regimen of root clipping, branch binding, and purposeful lack of feeding, a giant may be kept happy in a bowl no larger than one in which porridge is served.

5. Small stature might be the result of a chance mutation that would cause a young seedling to keep most of its parents' characteristics but become a short copy. These seedling mutations can often result in other changes affecting leaf color, shape, or size.

6. It may be small because of a "sport," or bud, mutation, where only one branch of a particular species gives evidence of any change. Thus instead of the embryo in a seed undergoing a genetic change causing the entire plant to change its appearance, only a comparatively few cells in one branch or twig change their programming. The result is a tree that might bear one touch of yellow within a mass of green or a few contorted needles where the others are long and straight. These bud mutations do not usually lead themselves to plants that can produce viable seed. Propagation of such sports is by asexual methods.

The well-known witches' broom is a variation on the bud mutation. This condition usually occurs on species of larch, spruce, or pine, where a tightly fisted batch of dwarf or congested needles will flare up on the tip of a normal tree branch. These growth variations are easily mistaken for bird's nests from a distance or, as folklore would see it, a witch's traveling aid.

Plants that are propagated by cuttings from broom branches grow into dwarf or small specimens, and many conifers now common in gardens were first cloned in this manner. Whatever the ultimate cause of a broom—mutation, insect attacks, or virus infections—the branches soon start to produce normal-size branches and ultimately kill the smaller ones by choking off all light and air.

SHAPES OF THE CONIFERS

In the world of small evergreens—conifers, to be specific—a number of shape definitions have evolved as a kind of horticultural shorthand. When listing plants, most catalogs specify—in addition to color of foliage and so on—a standard of shape: pyramidal, dwarf conical, prostrate, round, ovoid, columnar, rounded bush, weeping, or spreading. A particular plant will often have two or more of these attributes.
The following abbreviations will be used in this book:

UH, ultimate height. This is—or, in a few cases, thought to be—the final height a particular plant will reach.

US, ultimate spread. The same as UH, but in terms of outward growth.

AGR, annual growth rate. This refers to the increase in length on one branch. Thus a round bush with an AGR of five inches will increase its girth by ten inches.

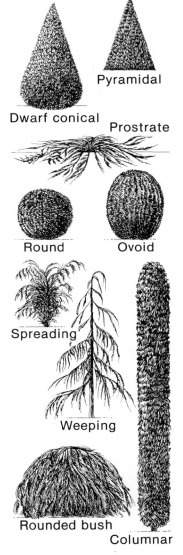

Pyramidal

Dwarf conical

Prostrate

Round   Ovoid

Spreading

Weeping

Rounded bush

Columnar

THE CASE FOR SMALL EVERGREENS

Time was when gardens covered vast acres, ringing estates with exotic colors and forms. They were fitting backgrounds for various social activities, and the plantings followed fashions that put a premium on rarity and reflected the owner's station in life. And those who saw these gardens would be classified into two groups: those who owned them (and their friends) and those who had to work in them.

Well, times have changed—much to the continual chagrin of some—and the days of the huge estate garden are mostly in the past. A few large gardens still remain as public parks, historic sites, or botanical research areas, supported by public or foundation funds. A few more survive as the suburban or country places of corporate executives, and, since the 1960s, a few are kept up in style by rock stars.

The vast majority of today's gardens, though, are small. One or two members of a family can maintain and develop them. Today's gardens range from a small terrace in the city to a few hundred square feet in the suburbs or an acre or two in the country.

Contributing to the shrinking size of gardens is the pattern of middle-class family life in the United States and Canada. One year will see a garden begin its development and the next the owner moving on to another job and starting all over again. Even older gardeners are often on the move; rising costs of keeping warm forces them into smaller homes and from the Frost Belt to the Sun Belt. And as the gardener advances in years, the physical effort of managing a large plot becomes more and more taxing. All in all, these trends argue for the smaller, self-contained, easily managed garden that will offer a continually changing picture over the seasons and years yet not outgrow its frame.

This is where the small evergreen makes its major contribution: It is small in the beginning and can be moved about with comparative ease and a reasonable minimum of backbreaking labor. If you give a little thought to planning, you can lay out your garden by leaving the plants in their original wraps or containers and moving them about the yard. Is this color right for here? Or how about here? And if you make a mistake, a small evergreen can be dug up and moved without a vast fleet of earth movers entering the scene.

There are, of course, other advantages. Small ever-greens do not require a great deal of space that must be reserved for later growth. They can and are easily ordered by mail, and they usually survive the rigors of packing and delivery. And, too, you need not wait for sixty years for the final effect: A few years with a small evergreen will give a satisfying result.

And, of course, the benefits of all evergreens can also be enjoyed in diminutive form: In spring they delight us with the flush of new growth; in summer the leaves mature and subtly change color; in fall many take on a new tone; and in winter they relieve the bleakness of the land—no bare branches here.

A FEW RULES FOR PLANNING AHEAD

One of the problems with writing about the making of gar-dens deals with the concept of rules. There are many people who like the clipped look and manicured neatness of an overly formal garden: all plants cut to size and neatly sur-rounded with leveled layers of mulch, perfectly raked dirt, and not a weed in sight. There appear to be people who manage to find the time to create a perfect garden and wish to be assured that their approach is the only correct ap-proach.

Their approach is not mine, however. Grass that is a few inches too long doesn't bother me until it begins to shroud the smaller plants at the garden's edge. Weeds, though not always welcome, do not incite fear and trembling in my psyche—at least not until they detract from the recognized plants in their neighborhood.

Another major piece of garden advice that has always left me cold is overattention to the supposed mismatching of colors. Of course, a tiny blossom of a light and delicate shell pink that measures a mere one-half inch in diameter would be lost among five rose bushes in full bloom, whatever the shade of their petals. But going out of your way to match flower colors as though you were painting an abstract water-color of various shades of blue is not my cup of tea.

That's not to say that I find one-color gardening as originally conceived by Gertrude Jekyll, the great English gardener, uninteresting. It can be splendid; the all-white garden planted by Vita Sackville-West at Sissinghurst in southern England is singularly beautiful. But never become a slave to one approach.

Now a few rules for small evergreen gardening:

1. Pay attention to the eventual size of a plant. Try to visualize what its girth will be five years from the day you plant it. Never plant a row of small shrubs that will eventually grow two feet high in front of a bush that will always ramble along a few inches above the soil.

2. Match the plant to the conditions available: Try to avoid putting a bush that requires perfect drainage next to another that will do fine in pure clay. The problem could be solved if you dig and move a great deal of earth, but why waste your efforts?

3. Avoid straight lines: They are never found in nature and at best are boring to look at—and intolerable to keep up. Also, they are most difficult to lay out to perfection. A gentle and sweeping curve looks far better and is much easier to maintain.

4. Trust your own aesthetic judgment. After all, it is your garden and should reflect your likes and color preferences, not those of some expert.

5. Stay away from garden ornaments that are not in scale with your garden. A small Japanese stone lantern—which can accommodate, as an added delight, a candle for evening viewing—would look much better in the average-size garden than would a six-foot marble statue of Apollo. If you want to acquire some garden sculpture, keep in mind the specific requirements of your own site. You will find that often scaled down ornaments add depth to a garden view rather than overpower it.

2.

Getting Ready

It's wonderful to have a well-designed and flourishing garden that only needs the addition of an evergreen or two to expand winter interest and give a new lift to your garden outlook year round. If that's your luck, merely look through Chapters 3 and 4 for suggestions of plants that might appeal.

But if you are just starting to work on a piece of unturned soil—an area of the yard that has been, up to now, open field; wasteland in general; old farmland that has reverted to brush; or the typical backyard left by subdivision developers—then the following suggestions should be helpful!

First, take paper and pencil and sketch a simple map of the area to be developed and planted. The map need not be complicated or picture perfect. It is not meant to stifle creativity; it just helps the gardener arrive at a general idea of

what he or she wishes to accomplish. Whether you have in mind a large garden of small conifers or a small, grassy verge surrounded by a bed of annuals with a few evergreens at center left, planning it all out beforehand saves time, energy, and grief.

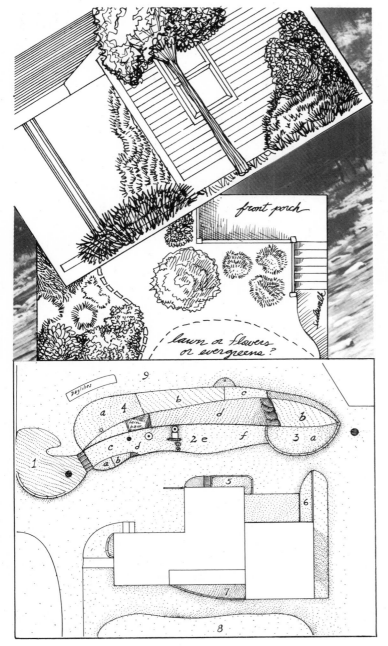

front porch

lawn or flowers
or evergreens?

A number of sketches and plans that describe various interpretations of garden layout. One shows the future growth of some evergreens by dotted lines; another uses the architect's drawing of a house and a felt-tip pen to suggest a layout; one is as rough as can be and another carefully thought out and labeled with a letter and number code; and even a photograph was used as a plan base with an india ink tree added by the owner.

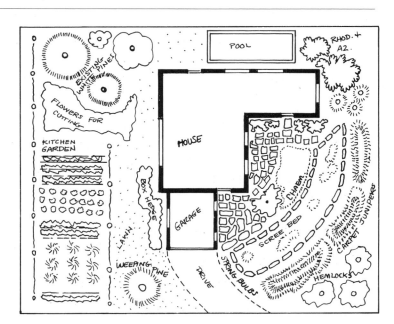

A few more layout samples including a candid photograph of a vacation home with inked-in evergreens and a detailed blueprint of a future landscape.

14

Decide how much land is to be cared for and how much time you will have for weeding and cultivating. Is your garden going to be a year-round pursuit or merely a sideline in the late spring and early fall? These are decisions that only the person who is going to do the work can make. And while you mull it over, remember that gardening always takes more time than you expect; nothing looks more dismal to you—or your neighbors--than an abandoned site with a few malnourished plants overwhelmed by weeds. In such cases it would have been better if the land had never been touched at all!

When you plan a site, refer to Chapter 3 for the ultimate spread of each plant you choose to work with and ALLOW ENOUGH ROOM FOR IT TO GROW! This last is in capitals because it's the first and easiest rule to be broken when planning any growing area. I know by experience the disasters that result when a gardener ignores this rule. Even true dwarf specimens will double their spread in ten years' time.

The empty spaces initially left between young bushes and trees for their future growth may be nicely filled with small groupings of annuals or perennials that are easily moved elsewhere as the primary specimens need more room.

As the plan is paced off, indicate the presence of natural windbreaks, existing trees, the direction of the worst winter winds, possible obstructions to spring and fall sunlight, and all structures—whether already there or planned for the future.

Checking the areas of such natural and artificial windbreaks is very important. You might find that your garden is in climate zone 5, since the lowest temperature of winter falls between $-20°$ and $-10°$F. But a plant that only survives in zone 6 or 7 when left in the open can thrive in zone 5 if it is planted in a spot that offers some shelter from brisk winter winds. With a planning map such spots are readily identified.

I have a small rhododendron that does beautifully every year even when temperatures fall to $-20°$F.—and those bitter temperatures are often joined by twenty-mile-an-hour winds. It is planted at the corner of our house just over the pipe that leads to the septic tank, and the soil there never freezes due to the constant warmth radiating from the tank and its plumbing.

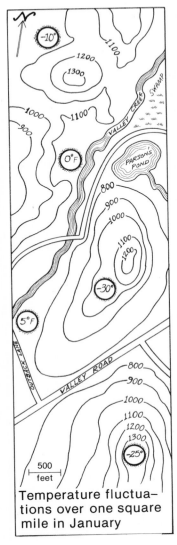

Temperature fluctua-
tions over one square
mile in January

CLIMATE ZONES

Speaking of temperature, this seems a good spot to talk about climate zones. You will find no map of the United States in this book depicting zones for annual high and low temperature, since I regard these as far more misleading than helpful.

To illustrate these zones clearly for the United States with any degree of accuracy, a chart two by four feet would be needed; small but absolutely critical differences in elevation never show up on book-size climate zone maps. In addition they can never take into account the wide variations in local climates that are created by such natural and artificial barriers as hills, ponds, and buildings, or the effects these objects have on the course of a wind that is whipping winter's chill.

This combination of wind and cold has hit the nation's weather forecasters as though it's a new invention of nature. They inform you that a balmy day in autumn with an air temperature of 40°F. can feel like 10°F. when the wind hits your face at forty miles per hour. Or step out on a sandy beach after a dip in the sea and an ocean breeze of fifteen knots will send the chills racing up and down your back. In either case the wind intensifies the cold you feel. Plants suffer the same chilling effect, but they cannot get up and move to a more protected spot! This combination of cold and wind is probably the single most important cause of winterkill; we'll keep reminding you of it when talking about selection and care of various plants in Chapter 3.

Just remember that when the wind blows about twenty-five miles per hour and the temperature outside is 0°F., the effect on your prized evergreen, if unprotected, is equivalent to −40°F. on a windless night. And no climate zone chart ever takes such temperatures into account.

In the following chart I have listed the temperatures in Fahrenheit. The metric system is a fine idea for standardizing worldwide industrial measurements, but I see no reason we must be forced to change the habits of generations and give up Fahrenheit for Celsius. No matter how much indoctrination I receive, 32° will always be when the pond starts to freeze, not a balmy summer afternoon.

**APPROXIMATE RANGE OF AVERAGE MINIMUM
TEMPERATURES (FAHRENHEIT) FOR EACH ZONE**

Zone 1	below	$-50°$
Zone 2	$-50°$ to	$-40°$
Zone 3	$-40°$ to	$-30°$
Zone 4	$-30°$ to	$-20°$
Zone 5	$-20°$ to	$-10°$
Zone 6	$-10°$ to	$0°$
Zone 7	$0°$ to	$10°$
Zone 8	$10°$ to	$20°$
Zone 9	$20°$ to	$30°$
Zone 10	$30°$ to	$40°$

SOIL TYPES

The plants I describe in this book—and all exceptions are noted—are far less demanding of good soils than are most other trees and garden perennials. But even the hardiest of them deserve some consideration when it comes to planting them in spots where they will remain the rest of their growing life.

When you start to plan a garden, your soil should be checked for its character. Is it solid clay; rich, beautiful, friable loam; or a combination of both? Is the soil well drained, or does water stand in puddles even after a light rain?

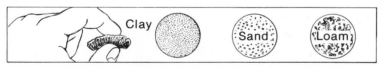

Clay soils are sticky. If you role a lump of wet soil between your fingers as if rolling a cigarette and it forms a compact cylinder that does not break up, that's clay. Clay can become rock hard when it is completely dry. Rather than sinking into the ground, water on dry clay soil simply rolls to the lowest level and sits.

All efforts should be directed toward preparing a garden soil that is a reasonable balance of clay, sand, and loam, so that the earth drains and roots do not sit in water. In addition there should be adequate food for the healthy development of the plants involved, and a pH that is reasonably acid.

17

CHECKING THE pH

pH is a method of measuring the relative acidity, or sourness, and alkalinity, or sweetness, of the soil. Every time it rains, the action of water washes out accumulations of elements in the soil. One of these elements is calcium, and as it disappears, the soil becomes more acidic. The process is extremely slow in nature, but over the years definite patterns of soil type will develop throughout any region. Swamps or bogs that have high percentages of peat are extremely acidic; in humid regions, and most woods and forests, the soil is moderately acidic to slightly alkaline; arid regions go from a slightly moderate to strong alkaline content; and desert areas in the Southwest have vast alkali flats.

The accompanying pH chart is a measure in units of 3 to 11. Neutral soil is 7. Most plants grow between ranges of 4.5 to 7.5.

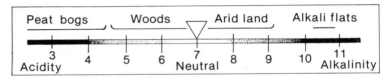

Garden centers now stock an inexpensive paper pH tape that can be held against moist soil. It turns various colors to indicate the degree of acidity. Since most evergreens do best in a soil that is at least moderately acidic, the average garden soil will be fine. If, however, your soil proves to be extremely alkaline, it is probably easier to grow evergreens in containers or fill special trenches with a proper soil mix rather than spend vast sums to truck in new loam and add pounds of peat. A few odd evergreens that prefer an alkaline soil are specifically pointed out in Chapter 3.

LIGHT

All plants need some light to survive and grow; evergreens require a great deal. Except for one or two exceptions—and they are noted in the cultural instructions—the plants described in this book require maximum light levels to insure their peak color intensity and healthy growth.

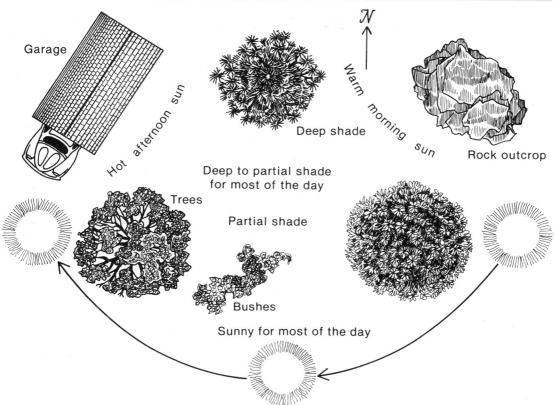

Even those small evergreens that require shade must have maximum sun in early spring; their shading becomes necessary when the hot summer sun of late June, July, and August combines with low summer rainfall to virtually bake the plants.

When you make a general map of your projected garden, make sure that the areas of full sun, half-day sun, and full shade are calculated for various seasons and clearly marked. Anticipate the shadows cast by buildings, large trees, shrubs, and rock outcrops. The following illustration shows a typical layout including the sun's path.

THE WAY PLANTS ARE SOLD

Because the final preparation of soil depends on the way evergreens are acquired for planting, the following definitions are important:

BALLED AND BURLAPPED: This is the way most nurseries sell evergreens of medium and large size. The roots are in a ball of earth that is wrapped with burlap—or often today a plastic, netlike material—to hold the soil firmly

19

Balled and
burlapped

Container grown

Bare root

around them and prevent them from drying out. As long as the root ball is watered with care, balled-and-burlapped plants can wait for weeks—even months—until their planting day. But when you water, make sure the ball is truly saturated; otherwise most of the water will roll down and off the wrapping.

CONTAINER-GROWN: Today many nurseries are using the container-grown approach to wholesale plant production. The plant to be sold is grown in its own pot—usually plastic—until it is ready to be planted by the customer. Time-release fertilizers are used by the nurseries so that the plants have steady nourishment. If properly cared for by the seller, such plants suffer much less transplant shock than those grown by the other methods. They can be planted almost anytime in the growing season and they usually survive. If you pop them into an attractive container, they can serve as temporary patio or terrace decorations until final planting.

Container-grown plants are also easy to ship by mail or UPS. If a plant is delayed in transit, the presence of the dirt and pot keep the roots from drying out completely.

BARE-ROOT: Very young trees and bushes not more than two or three years old may be shipped as bare-root plants. The soil is removed from the roots and they are then lightly wrapped with a ball of moist sphagnum moss or shredded wood and paper strips that are thoroughly soaked just prior to shipping out.

When received, they require immediate care. Open the package to see that the moss has not dried out and place the plants in a cool, shady spot. Give the opened package a thorough soaking in a pail of muddy water for at least twenty-four hours before planting. If you can't get to the job right away, bare-root plants should be heeled in.*

There are variations on the foregoing shipping methods, but any responsible supplier will enclose a packing slip that specifies how to care for the plants with each shipment.

---

*When bare-root plants are received, remove the waterproof packing. Dig a shallow trench, about six inches deep, and place the plants on their sides two or three inches apart at an angle of 45°. Water well. Then heel the dirt back over the roots. Never put plants in a bucket of water for days on end, thinking you will get to them tomorrow; the roots will rot.

DOUBLE DIGGING

Once your planting scheme is settled, the time arrives for actually working the soil. If you are one of the lucky few who are blessed with a perfect site and perfect soil, or if you merely wish to add a few plants to an existing garden, pass this section by. If not . . .

First clear the ground of all existing weeds or grass with a mower or scythe, raking them into piles for later use at the bottom of the trenches you will dig. The following figure shows the general idea.

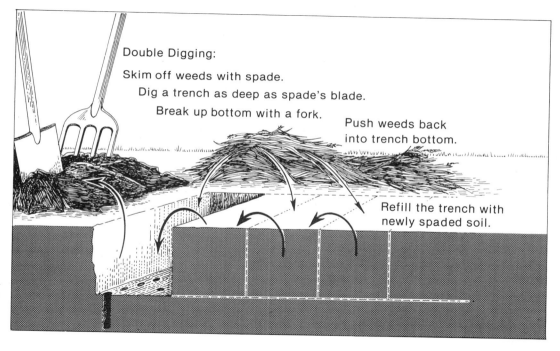

Double Digging:

Skim off weeds with spade.

Dig a trench as deep as spade's blade.

Break up bottom with a fork.

Push weeds back into trench bottom.

Refill the trench with newly spaded soil.

Don't use a rototiller; the idea of double digging is to replace the subsoil with a better quality of fill, not just to work the surface soil about. Such surface tilling is only for soil that has already been sufficiently worked.

The foregoing caveat is only for those people who are starting out from scratch and are putting in an entire garden, not just adding a few plants to an existing spread. But remember, if ever there were a time for a gardener to be an ant and not a grasshopper, soil preparation is the time. Once finished, the worst is over; all future planting will be a breeze.

PLANTING OUT

Once the soil is prepared, the planting can begin. Use the following steps for each tree, whether in a container or balled.

1. Dig a hole that allows about six inches' space all around the root ball. Put the excavated soil to one side. If you are planting in an existing lawn, put the soil on top of a tarpaulin or piece of burlap so that when you are finished, everything can once again be neat and orderly. Always plan on a larger hole than you think you need: The old adage is, Never put a ten-dollar tree in a five-dollar hole.

2. Dump a pailful of well-rotted or composted manure into the bottom of the hole and work it in; never use raw commercial fertilizers or fresh manure, since either will burn the roots of the plant. If the plant is large and the trunk is weak, now is the time to add a stake for future support. This is usually not a problem with most evergreens, but some bare-root specimens might need a few months to take hold and the additional support could be valuable.

3. Take the excavated soil and mix it, if needed, with peat moss and sharp or builder's sand, not beach sand.* Use four parts of the soil to one part peat and one part sand. Proportions need not be absolutely perfect.

4. Place the ball in the hole so that the ground level reaches the point it did where the tree originally stood. Do not remove the burlap; it will rot over the years. Just remove any wrapping that would stick out in the open air above the soil level; otherwise the material would act like a wick and draw moisture from the soil, thence to be evaporated, especially when the wind is blowing. If the wrap is plastic, it should be removed, but wait until the earth ball is in place before you cut most of it away. The idea of all this care is to keep from disturbing the tiny rootlets that absorb water and nutrients so that they can continue to do their job efficiently. If the plant is in a container, make sure the root ball is moist, then carefully remove it.

Occasionally the gardener may buy a plant that has spent too many seasons in one container, never having grad-

*Builder's sand, which is used for mixing concrete, has sharp edges so that the grains never mass up in compact balls. Beach sand has been worn away by the action of waves; the grains are round and smooth and easily pack down, thus preventing good drainage and aeration of the roots.

uated to a larger size when needed. The evidence will be that the main roots grow in a circle around the inner wall of the container. Do not plant it this way. Unwind the roots and spread them about in the hole. Otherwise, the main roots will continue to grow in a circled path, never radiating out naturally to support the plant.

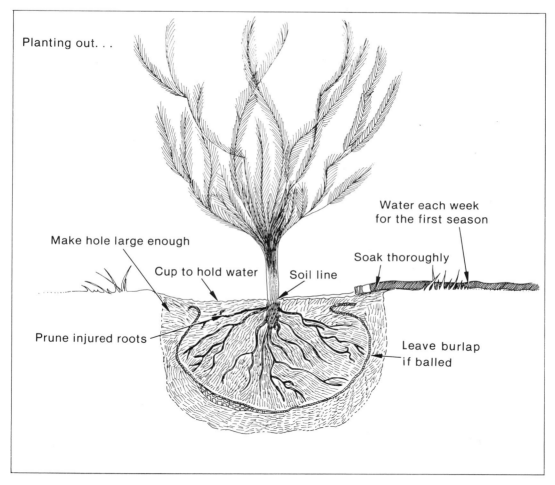

Planting out. . .

Make hole large enough

Cup to hold water

Soil line

Water each week for the first season

Soak thoroughly

Prune injured roots

Leave burlap if balled

5. Fill the remaining hole with water. Let it settle, then firmly pack the soil about the roots and push it down tight. Use your fingers and keep mashing that mucky soil down. This is another important time in planting. If it's not properly seated in the soil, the plant will never do well. Air pockets left under or around the ball are sure death for fragile rootlets. Leave a slight lip at the edge of your digout to act as a catch basin for water.

Try to pick a planting time just after a soaking spring rain, preferably on a cloudy day. Some authorities advise spraying foliage with a chemical antiwilt preparation, but I've never found it necessary if care is taken with the initial planting. Don't panic if you see some wilting; evergreens are very strong by nature and can take some transplant shock.

Continue to water during the rest of the growing season. Too often a person chooses the planting well and prepares the ground with care, and then overlooks subsequent waterings and the plant dries up for good. Extra care in watering is crucial during the plant's first summer while the new roots settle in and overcome the inevitable trauma—no matter how slight—of transplanting.

If the plants are received as a bare-root shipment, soak the roots well, adding dirt to the pail of water so that they truly soak in mud. Make sure that the hole is well prepared and the soil moist. Spread the roots out and firm the soil well, using your fingers and hands for packing. Stake when needed. Mulch well to prevent excess drying and be doubly sure of careful watering the first season.

Once the plant is in the ground, it's there—you hope—for the rest of its long life; dirt can be loosened and fertilizer added, but the initial care determines the course of growth.

Three years ago last spring, I planted a "Skyrocket" juniper beyond most of our plantings. The tree was nursery-dug and well wrapped and balled when delivered. I dug a large hole and planted the tree with well-tended soil and a lot of water. Every week that summer I hauled the hose over to the new tree and soaked the soil. My wife questioned the need for so much well water in a dry year, but I persisted. The tree is now beautiful and thriving: All that water insured a good start.

RECORD KEEPING

Labeling does not seem important when stacked up against tilling, plowing, digging, planting, weeding, and all the other hard work of gardening, but it is a valuable activity nonetheless. There seems to be an inherent desire in all human beings, but particularly plant people, to know the correct name of everything. Specific information about every one of your plants is a great thing to have at your fingertips when taking friends and family on a garden tour. If you plan on selling or trading any plants in the future, records become doubly important.

All you need is a simple three-by-five-inch card file with space on each card for the scientific and common name, the date of acquisition and the age of the plant, the nursery or plant supplier, a few general hints on care, a space for future notes on attempts at propagation, and anything else about this particular plant needed for the record.

BOTANICAL NAME *Pinus Mugo var. Mugo*			
COMMON NAME *Swiss Mountain Pine*	FAMILY *Pinaceae*		
SOURCE *Bold's garden center*	LABELED *plastic*		
REC'D AS *plant*	DAY / MON / YEAR *5 6 79*	LOCATION *rock garden*	

PROPAGATION

Cuttings made Sept. '79. Two rooted. Lost three Moved May '81 to enlarge garden; Fine in Aug9

At the same time a durable label should be prepared for the plant. Plastic labels or stakes soon crack and shatter, especially in a typical northern winter. They also heave out of the ground with winter thaws and, once free, the wind will blow them far and wide. Try instead the metal labels provided with long wire supports and mark the names by scratching the labels with a nail or knife; wooden labels with the names painted on and then varnished for additional protection; the Dymo® Tapewriters that print names on a glued vinyl strip; or, for the ultimate in labels, the Dymo® model 1011, which embosses on stainless steel or aluminum tape.

CONTINUING CARE

Once the evergreen is in the ground, the time comes for continual care. Here is a checklist of points I've found useful:

1. Winter cold combined with winter sun will cause troublesome heaving of unprotected or unmulched ground. The ground alternately freezes and thaws, forcing up shallow-rooted or newly planted trees and plants and exposing roots to wind and sun. This is a major problem where there is little snowfall in a normal winter; snow is probably the best protection that a plant can have. It acts as a perfect insulation barrier.

Exposed roots must be promptly pushed down into the soil again before the plant is permanently injured. Your heel gently but firmly applied, is an excellent tool.

Winter mulching is the best prevention. It does not protect the roots directly, but it does keep the ground firmly frozen until the final warmth of spring.

2. Promptly remove all weeds growing close to the evergreens, and keep all grass at least one foot away from the outside edge of any tree or shrub planted in your lawn. Grass and weeds take nourishment—and sunlight—away from small trees.

3. Cover all exposed earth with a mulch—well-composted manure, shells, wood chips, pine needles, pine branches, or even crushed gravel—to inhibit future weed growth and conserve moisture. Do not use sawdust, grass clippings, or peat moss: They pack down too tightly and, in the case of peat moss, will actually repel water when dry.

4. Top-dress trees that have been unattended for a year or two by spreading a thin layer (one to two inches) of a mix of soil and/or peat mixed two to one with well-rotted manure. This should be worked into the earth under the tree and extended slightly beyond the circumference of the overhanging branches.

5. If you want to help an older tree that shows signs of neglect, try the spiking method. Walk out to the drip edge of the tree—slightly beyond the tips of overhanging branches—and with a crowbar, punch a series of one-foot deep holes, one foot apart, along an imaginary circle. Fill the holes with a mixture of the top dressing just described. With small trees it isn't much fuss, but when you are dealing with large and old trees, the spiking process can be a major workout. I once revived two large, old apple trees, but couldn't punch holes since there were more rocks in the soil than dirt. I was forced to excavate to the diameter of a one-pound coffee can. My toil was rewarded; the trees have substantially increased their apple crop.

6. Remove dead branches with a sharp running saw or shears, coating wounds with such dressing products as Treekote® or Cabot's Tree Healing Paint®. Please use the brush-on types; stay away from the aerosol types. Lawn mowers, pets, and people can easily break branches and even scrape bark off the trunk. You might consider low fencing for your more treasured specimens.

7. Evergreens, unlike herbaceous plants and trees, can suffer from drought during the first year of being planted out. The needlelike leaves can lose moisture through the combined actions of cold and winter winds and are unable to replace it, since the roots are sealed fast in the frozen earth.

To lessen the possibility of drought you can improvise screens for protection against winter winds. Even an old Christmas tree can be propped up next to small evergreens to deflect the wind. Burlap stapled to wooden stakes surrounding the specimen will work well. Good carpenters often construct small pyramids of wooden slats that are set over plants—wooden tents that are taken out of storage every autumn, year after year.

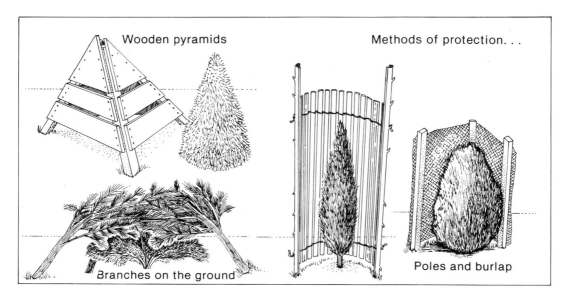

Wooden pyramids

Methods of protection. . .

Branches on the ground

Poles and burlap

If a particular tree is an experiment and truly belongs to a warmer climate, a screen can usually help it survive the winter. Remember to put the foundation stakes of such a windscreen around the plant before the ground freezes up. But wait until the end of autumn before wrapping the burlap around the specimen. And in a dry autumn, water each tree liberally before the ground does freeze solid.

8. Anticipate the ravages of deer, dogs, rabbits, and mice. Deer in many parts of the country, especially in the outer suburbs and abandoned farms of the Northeast, are enjoying a population revival. When winters are bad and natural food is short—or even when winters are reasonably mild and food is plentiful in the woods—these marauding Bambis will move right in and rape, pillage, and destroy: They prefer the ease of eating in a garden to anything that the wild will provide. It's no joke to lavish hours of care on a particular plant only to come out in the morning to find it nibbled to the ground, needles and all. And remember, wildlife fans, that deer, chipmunks, mice, rabbits, woodchucks, and so forth will continue to chew anything available even if you've left them plenty of food.

A number of suggestions have been advanced to deal with the deer problem. A dog can help, but only when it is trained to patrol the property's perimeter continually and stays outdoors most of the time. Deer soon learn when the dog is about and plan their forages for the times when it isn't. On the other hand, dogs can swiftly kill any tree or plant they adopt for a green hydrant, not to mention the damage they can do merely by running through a backyard at top speed. Nylon stockings made into small bags and filled with human hair clippings and then hung on trees like Christmas tree ornaments are the newest suggestion made by the various state conservation departments, but the final vote on this method has yet to be tabulated. Applications of human urine along the perimeter of the garden is another suggestion that is reputed to repel the deer—but only meat eaters need apply, since vegetarian urine apparently does not offend (and the application of this remedy would seem to repel most gardeners, too). And finally there is fencing.

Fencing is probably the best bet. For small gardens or a few plants and trees, compact cages made of wire fencing—rabbit, hog, or the new tomato wire work well—will stand up against most animals, last for years, and each cage is merely taken up and stored during the summer months. Chicken wire is left out of this list, since it is too weak to stand alone and requires the construction of some framework to complete the cage.

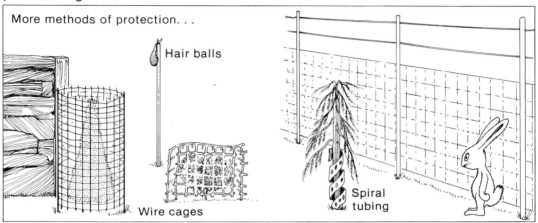

More methods of protection. . .

Hair balls

Wire cages

Spiral tubing

In my garden I've surrounded the perimeter with seven-foot-high metal posts—the type used by most farmers to hold wooden snow fencing. These are spaced about ten feet apart and hold wire fencing that is four feet high, which does a good job in keeping out small animals. I then tie white twine—called surveyor's or transit twine—from one post to the next, at a five-foot and a seven-foot height. I don't know why it works, but it does; the deer walk right up to the twine, sniff it carefully, but so far have refused to jump over.

Tree trunks can also be covered with plastic trunk protectors made of flexible tubing, punched with small holes for ventilation, and cut along a spiral, enabling the gardener to twine them around the trunk to give protection from rabbits and mice.

Mice can be discouraged if you keep surrounding grass cut short and weed piles to a minimum, but the best solution is to keep a cat. Our feline, Miss Jekyll, does a yeowoman's job of keeping the mouse population down in the confines of the garden.

Finally, nothing discourages wildlife more than the gardener taking early morning or late evening walks in the garden, such unscheduled meanderings generally upsetting the precise scheduling of most animals. I often go out just before sunrise and enjoy the sound of deer snorting in rage because a human is in the vicinity.

PRUNING

Most varieties of evergreens need no pruning to improve their shape; their natural form is usually attractive from the start. Occasionally, however, a plant will grow too large for its location, and the gardener finds that it cannot be moved without great difficulty. If this happens, vigorous pruning of the branches—early spring is the best time—on an annual basis will keep the tree to the desired size.

Another case for pruning is when the trunk and main branches are obscured by heavy growth of secondary branches on the outer parts of the tree; the visual interest of the tree can often be improved when these outer branches are thinned. And on older trees, you may want to remove the lowest branches that are resting on the ground to facilitate weeding, mowing, and the like.

When there is winter damage, the offending branch should be removed. Sometimes the thickness of needle growth on the branch ends deprive the undergrowth of sufficient light. These inner twigs eventually die and should be removed.

Always use a sharp and clean knife, saw, or sharp pruning shears. Never just break off a branch on your way through the garden. Nine times out of ten, small wounds will never become infected, but it isn't worth taking the chance. If the wound is over the diameter of a dime, apply a bit of wound dressing, using a flattened stick or tongue depresser for the applicator.

If you must move a dwarf or small conifer and you cannot find or afford a Vermeer tree-moving machine, you need to prune the roots. Circle the tree with deep spade cuts a year before you plan to move it, thus encouraging new and healthy root growth closer to the tree's center. Then when you do move it, the tree settles in with an extra lease on life.

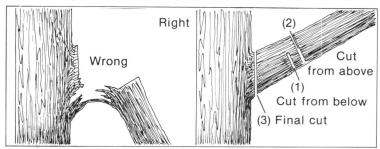

Wrong

Right

(2)

Cut from above

(1)
Cut from below

(3) Final cut

PESTS

It's much easier to work with and protect the majority of small conifers and evergreens from disease than cure them once a problem has set in. But except for animal ravaging we've mentioned before, these plants are usually not too susceptible to debilitating diseases.

Aphids and caterpillars can be controlled with a couple of weekly applications of any handy garden spray insecticide. Spider mites, one of the worst pests, are smaller than a pinhead, but their presence is detected by the tiny webs they spin over and around the needles and the eventual yellowing of the foliage. Hosing plants with jets of water should keep mites under control: mites cannot abide water and only seem to flourish during pronounced dry spells.

Gypsy moths can be a vexing problem. Though they prefer other comestibles to needles and tough evergreen leaves such as the rhododendron's, as a last resort they will, when all other food is gone, devour anything in their path: I have seen rhododendron leaves turned into a mesh of naked midribs. Since conifers cannot produce a second crop of leaves, as deciduous trees can; they can be lost forever.

When gypsy moth caterpillars are very young, trees can be sprayed with Dipel®, a concentration of bacterial spores that infect the pests so they cannot digest food. Older caterpillars resist infection longer and thus destroy a great deal of foliage before they themselves expire. Larger trees can be helped if you surround the trunks a few feet above the ground with a burlap strip soaked in tanglefoot—a sticky mess that traps the worms.

If your trees are too large to spray by hand and lie within an area of major gypsy moth defoliation, the best bet then is to hire a professional spraying outfit. They can protect your trees with heavy-duty spray equipment whether by truck or plane.

Your best offense, however, is to examine the trunks and branches of the trees in your garden during the winter, looking for the egg cases of the moths. These will be light brown fuzzy masses about two inches long and one-half inch wide. Coat each mass with a bit of wound dressing or scrape them off into a can for burning. Merely tossing them on the ground will not work; they will only hatch there in the spring.

Take the opportunity to walk about your garden whenever you can and examine each plant so that you are aware of an insect or pest invasion as soon as it occurs.

PROPAGATION OF EVERGREENS

Two general methods are used for the propagation of evergreens (both gymnosperms and angiosperms): seeds and cuttings. Cuttings include the processes of layering and grafting, though grafting is best left to the nursery professional, since the percentage of failure for the amateur can be quite disheartening.

SEEDS: About the only personality trait required to grow most evergreens from seed is patience. To begin with, all the hardy or semihardy evergreen conifer seeds must have periods of dormancy at a temperature of 40°F.—or less—for two to three months before germination begins. If nature had not given seeds this internal clock, they could germinate in the fall and send a tiny plant up through the snow only to face three to six months of freezing weather and certain death. After the seed has germinated, the gardener might have to wait up to three years—depending on the species—until the tiny plant is mature enough to face the rigors of an unprotected life out of doors. Even then the job isn't over, since still small trees need added protection from heavy snow, animals, and even human feet.

On the other hand, there is a certain excitement in seeing the first touch of green and knowing you made the necessary environment that enabled the seed to germinate.

And to make the gardener's job a little easier, all of today's seed packs give full and complete instructions on the dormancy required and general steps needed to insure satisfactory germination.

When seeds arrive, or are gathered, store them until you are ready to plant them in clean jars or plastic bags clearly labeled with the name of each species and the source of the seed. Put the packs in a cool spot—60°F. or less, away from radiators or excess heat.

As I've mentioned, most evergreen conifers require a period of cold dormancy before they will sprout.* Unless instructions tell you differently, place the seeds when you're ready to start in a slightly moist, but not wet, mixture of sand and/or sphagnum moss. Put this mix in a small jar or plastic baggie with the top tightly sealed and store in the refrigerator for three months. This time period should cover the requirements of most of the evergreens, whether conifers or flowering plants.

When the three months have passed, the seeds and the mix can then be sown as a unit on a sterile growing medium such as Park's Sow 'n Grow® or a medium of your own creation; milled sphagnum moss, peat moss, and sand in equal amounts will do fine.

Containers to grow seedlings can be almost as varied as your imagination: cardboard milk or cream containers, frozen orange juice cans, coffee cans, egg cartons, or commercial peat pots will all do the job. The only requirement common to them all is a need for perfect drainage. Seeds, unless aquatic in origin, will quickly rot in an overly wet mix.

AVERAGE REFRIGERATOR TIMES FOR CONIFER SEEDS

Cedrus (cedar)	1–2 months
Chamaecyparis (false cypress)	2
Picea (spruce)	1–3
Pine (most species)	2
Thuja (arborvitae)	2
Tsuga (hemlock)	3

We know that seeds need water for germination, but they also need oxygen from the air for life processes to begin. If we are too heavyhanded, the mix will be so wet that the seeds will be completely surrounded by water; no oxygen will

---

*Among the flowering evergreens, the following require no dormant periods but may be sown directly as gathered or held until the following spring: azaleas, *erica, kalmia, leucothoe,* and the rhododendrons.

be available to the embryo plant and it will die. This is the reason why overwatering of seeds is to be avoided at all costs.

If you have collected the seeds yourself, or if the seed package neglected to give you the information, and you are worried about how deep to plant the seeds, use the following rule to determine planting depth: seeds, one-sixteenth inch or larger, should be covered by the thickness of one seed; tiny seeds need not be covered at all but just settled in with a light spray of water from a hand mister. When sowing seeds, use a folded piece of paper, tapping it gently as you move it across the surface.

Generally, fill your containers close to the top, leaving a quarter inch or less to the container edge. This performs two functions: It allows for freer circulation of air, thus inhibiting the growth of surface molds, and it makes you more aware of the fledgling plants when watering.

Tamp the growing mix down and proceed to wet it thoroughly. Pour water over the top with care: don't pour water from a great height or use the faucet at full force; you wish to wet and settle the mix, not agitate it. Drain well for at least an hour before you plant.

Another way to wet the seeding medium is to put the contents in a bowl, add water, stir well, and squeeze the excess water out with your hands. Then place it in containers.

Once seeds are planted, cover the containers with plastic wrap or panes of glass. Be careful to keep plastic wrap away from the surface; a plant label or small stake can serve as a tiny tent pole. If you don't, drops of moisture will condense—especially if you are using a heating cable—fall down on the seeds as heavy drops and form small swamps. This miniature greenhouse will prevent the medium from drying out, an event to be avoided at all costs. Once germination begins, smaller seeds especially must never be allowed to dry out. Put the containers in a warm spot away from the direct rays of the sun. Soon they will want all the available sun, but not until they sprout. Heating cables placed under the growing mix will generate enough heat to insure germination. They are available from most mail-order nursery suppliers and from many garden centers.

When the first green shoots appear, move the containers into the direct sunlight. On the other hand, if you're doing this during the late spring or summer, caution must be taken with the very hot rays of the midday sun; you should use some protection such as screening. Turn your plants to keep them from bending to the light. Remove the plastic or glass covering and check on the water situation at least twice a day. When the mix starts to dry, either water from the bottom through the drainage holes or from the top with a mister. A water bulb used to sprinkle laundry before ironing works very well.

Upon germination your seedlings will have two needles or leaves. When more develop and grow, it's time to apply a liquid fertilizer, such as Hyponex® or Miracle Grow®, to make up for the lack of nutrients in the mix. Follow instructions on the package, then dilute the solution by half. Even if you are using soil, the applications of such a solution will not endanger the plants.

You can now transplant to small peatpots or, if you are leaving the plants in their original flats or containers a while longer, thin them—if needed—allowing at least one inch between plants. Small plants should remain in the original container until they are large enough for you to handle with comparative ease.

The pointed end of a knife or a plastic plant label makes an excellent tool for transplanting. Just be gentle! Pick up the plant and lightly cover the roots with soil that is damp, not mucky.

Plants should be moved into three-inch clay or plastic pots when they are about three inches high.

The following rules should help in any seed project:

1. Don't overwater, mix should be kept moist not wet.
2. Never let the growing mix dry out.
3. Water gently to prevent disturbing tiny seeds and plants.
4. Never sow seeds too deep. If in doubt, just cover them with a light layer of mix.
5. Keep seeds from direct sunlight until germination is complete. If seeds sprout in late spring or summer, always give small plants additional protection with a piece of screening or a light curtain at the window. Without constant watching, small containers dry quickly.

As a general rule, I have not planted out any evergreen seedlings until the third year of growth. During the winter

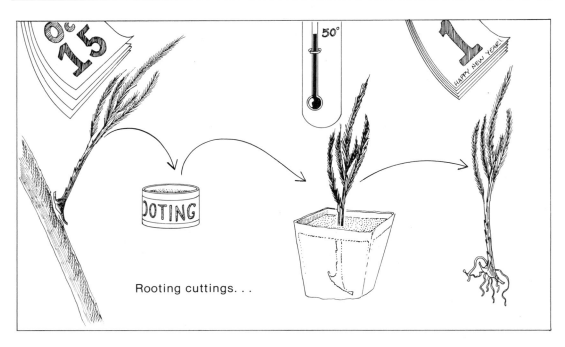

Rooting cuttings. . .

months, I keep young plants in my greenhouse at a temperature of 35°F. on some cold nights. Water is given only when the soil is completely dry.

CUTTINGS. If we had to wait for nurseries to grow all the desired plants from seed, there would never be enough to go around. Luckily, nature has provided a method to produce more plants: asexual, or vegetative, reproduction. This is a process that gives most plants the ability to produce—or clone—offspring from special cells found in leaves, stems, and roots.

It is best to root cuttings in the late autumn or early winter. Wait for one or two nights of frost before you proceed. Cuttings should be taken from twigs approximately eighteen months old—not new growth from the present year's spring. The cutting should be a minimum of six inches long and include a heel or a small section of the older wood found at the cutting's base where the chosen twig joins the parent branch. Dip the bottom end in a hormone powder made specifically for rooting. Hormex Rooting Powders® sell one strength of hormone for conifer settings and another for hardwood evergreen cuttings. Many attempts at rooting cuttings work well without the addition of these hormones, but they often give the grower an extra edge at success.

A rooting medium of moist sand and peat moss or sand and milled sphagnum* is best. Moist, not soaking wet. You can then use almost any container that will hold your cutting without toppling over. I generally stick with peat pots, since they can eventually be planted pot and all.

Insert the cutting up to one half its length and pack the medium around the stem. Now put the cuttings in a protected spot shaded from strong sunlight and at a temperature between 45° and 60°F. Keep the medium moist at all times.

Those cuttings that root—do not be discouraged with failure but try again—can be planted out the following spring and treated like any young plant. Rooting action should begin within eight weeks of starting the process.

Expanding a collection of evergreens by asexual propagation is the only way for the supply to keep up with the demand, but it is not always the easiest thing to succeed at. For those interested in this method of reproduction I recommend the book *Plant Propagation* by John P. Mahlstede and Ernest S. Haber published by John Wiley & Sons, Inc.

CONTAINER GARDENING

One of the charms of the smaller evergreen conifers, azaleas, and rhododendrons is the comparative ease with which they can be grown in containers. And especially for those gardeners in the city who have nothing but a terrace or small lot in the suburbs, container gardening is a most satisfying pastime.

A container by definition could vary from a small pot to a sunken soapstone sink to a large, raised bed in the backyard constructed of fieldstone or brick. They will all have one thing in common: the dirt they contain will be mixed to your specifications and can be adjusted far more readily than an entire lot of poor soil.

The decorative possibilities of container gardening are almost endless. I have an especially fine dwarf redwood (*Sequoia sempervirens* 'Adpressa') that is much too tender to withstand our rugged winters. By planting it in a terracotta

*Milled sphagnum is sphagnum moss that has been shredded into tiny pieces, making it much easier than the unmilled variety to work with and mix with other ingredients.

pot, it becomes an attractive addition to my rock garden when it sits atop the wall or can be moved to the terrace to sit among pots of blooming annuals. Then in the fall it stands by the front door and for Christmas, a few decorations are added, and we have a living holiday tree.

There is but one requirement: plants in small containers will do best if sunk in the ground for the winter and allowed to endure the cold with the rest of outdoor nature. If they are brought under shelter, they must have at least three months at an average temperature of no more than 40° to 45°F. Without meeting these conditions, the plants will die; they must have a sustained period of dormancy once a year.

If a potted plant is left outside without being buried or given other protection, the bitter winds striking the pots will soon kill the plants' roots. If the winds don't kill the plant, the repeated freezing and thawing of the soil in smaller pots will do the job just as surely.

If you live in the colder parts of the country, there is the additional problem of clay pots that break when the water in their pores freezes and expands, so the best thing to do is use plastic pots that can rest within larger and more decorative containers.

When a small evergreen must be brought indoors because there is no way of providing adequate protection outside, there is an additional problem to be considered. Even though you have the facilities to store the plant at the required temperature of 40° to 45°F., you now have to remember to water occasionally. Since the soil about the plant's roots is not frozen solid, the roots continue to draw small amounts of water—they do not stop activity completely. The container must be watered every three or four weeks. The soil cannot be allowed to become bone dry. This must not be overlooked. Evergreens do not evidence wilt as quickly as most other plants; by the time the damage is in evidence, it's usually too late to cure.

LARGER CONTAINERS

If you are fortunate enough to find one of the old soapstone laundry tubs you will have a perfect above-ground container for a small garden. These tubs are large enough to stand outside through a northern winter and give protection to the plants within. Some of the larger nursery outlets have started to cast large concrete tubs in nineteenth-century shapes with cherubs chasing gargoyles about the edges.

But even a large modern porcelain laundry tub can be covered with a mixture of hypertuffa and make a fine addition to the garden. Hypertuffa is made of equal parts of cement, fine peat moss, and builder's sand in equal quantities. It gives the weathered look of old stone. And by building wooden frames of varying dimensions, countless varieties of large pots, troughs, and tubs can be manufactured with ease.

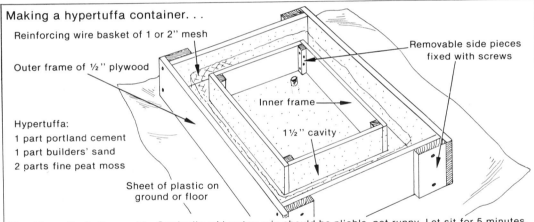

Making a hypertuffa container. . .

Reinforcing wire basket of 1 or 2" mesh

Outer frame of ½" plywood

Removable side pieces fixed with screws

Inner frame

Hypertuffa:
1 part portland cement
1 part builders' sand
2 parts fine peat moss

1½" cavity

Sheet of plastic on ground or floor

Blend ingredients thoroughly. Gradually add water; mix should be pliable, not runny. Let sit for 5 minutes. Put 1" layer in frame and set in armature, equal distance from all sides. Add cement to make 1½" deep layer all over bottom then set the inner frame in place. Set wooden plugs for drains. Fill rest of cavity. Lay plastic over top. In 12 to 18 hours remove inner frame, carefully pull out plugs and remove sections. Replace plastic cover. 24 hours later remove outer form. Brush sides and top with bristled brush. Wrap in plastic for 3 more days. Clean drainage holes. Wrap again and let cure for 2 more weeks. Then expose to several rainstorms.

If you are making your own hypertuffa container from scratch, you can provide adequate drainage holes in the bottom. If you are using one of the old sinks, the existing drainage hole must be clear and the bottom quarter of the container filled with a mixture of small stones, broken crocks, or gravel before the soil mix is added.

A good soil mix for such a container would be equal parts of good garden loam or topsoil, well-rotted or composted manure, shredded peat moss, and builder's sand. Many of the smaller evergreens described in the next chapter would be quite at home in such a container garden. If you are in an area of heavy snowfall, small plants can be protected by providing a topping of carefully placed evergreen branches or a cover held above the plants by resting it on stones set below the corners.

A LARGER ABOVE-GROUND BED

In addition to the sink or trough garden, with some hard work—and hopefully the use of a backhoe or tractor accompanied by a friend or handyman—a dry wall can be constructed to rise above your present ground level to a height of one, two, or three feet, depending on the lay of your land. When filled with a mix of soil, peat moss, sand, and crushed stone, a perfect planting bed is formed—in scale with many of the smaller evergreens and giving them ideal drainage.

Our backyard was made up of red shale with a superficial cover of pure clay. Though it was able to support the more common annuals and perennials—only when spiked with new soil and humus—the planting of small evergreens in such barren soil would never have worked. In addition, the rear of the yard rises up in an eight-foot-high bank that in turn joins a more gradual rise to the fields above. And that bank was made years ago with more clay, shale, and rock to protect the living quarters of our house from chill winter winds.

I built a semi-circular three-foot dry wall of fieldstone in the corner of the backyard. Each end of the wall circles about to run directly into the bank behind. Since the average fieldstone used was one and one-half to two feet wide and four to six inches thick, the wall has great stability; one can sit on the edge with comfort and look at the smaller plants just below eye level.

We are now going into the third winter enjoying this enormous container. Since the underlying stones were set with great care, there has been a minimum of settling and only a few of the outer stones have shifted.

New fill of gravel, peat moss, and composted or dried manure

Existing hill

Rock wall

Rubble

A scree garden for dwarf conifers

Besides being filled with a variety of small evergreens and rock garden plants, the spaces between the stones themselves have been used to grow a number of diminutive flowers and succulents, such as sedums and sempervivums.

Where old stone walls are not available for dismantling or stone is expensive, the height of such a bed can be kept to twelve to sixteen inches and still offer all sorts of prospects.

3.

The Small Conifers

The small evergreens described in this chapter are chosen with a biased viewpoint: not only do most of them appeal to me—would that I could own them all!—but they are at this writing available from the nurseries listed in Chapter 5. When assembling a list of the specimens chosen for description in this book, I tried to anticipate the frustrations of readers who, embarking on a conifer career, dutifully write for catalogs and visit garden centers and nurseries, only to find a large percentage of their choices unavailable.

I patiently went over the mail-order sources known to me and picked those plants for inclusion that appear in two or more listings. In fact, most of those mentioned are offered by three or more firms.

The botanical nomenclature is as clear as I could manage in a field that is best described as confused. If a choice existed between two names—from indecision on the part of the scientific community or some other reason—I've listed both names.

General growing conditions precede each group. And growth figures, based on the various sources listed in the bibliography or my own observations or those of fellow growers and gardeners, are given whenever they are avail-

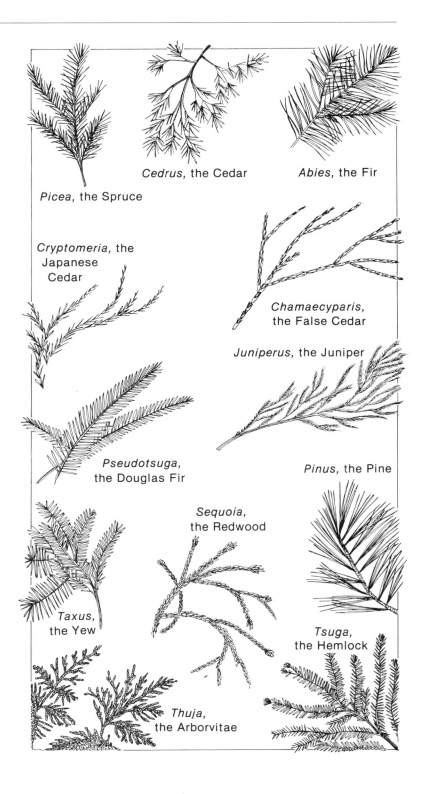

Picea, the Spruce

Cedrus, the Cedar

Abies, the Fir

Cryptomeria, the Japanese Cedar

Chamaecyparis, the False Cedar

Juniperus, the Juniper

Pseudotsuga, the Douglas Fir

Pinus, the Pine

Sequoia, the Redwood

Taxus, the Yew

Tsuga, the Hemlock

Thuja, the Arborvitae

able. Before planting anything check the information compiled in Chapter 2.

I must emphasize that this book is not meant to be a scientific treatise on evergreens, nor is it meant to be a definitive volume on these plants. What I've aimed for is to introduce the reader to the marvelous facets of gardening with these beautiful plants and point out the wide range of possibilities they provide.

Climate zones given are approximate, as I have discussed in Chapter 2. Invariably when I list a plant as suitable only for zone 6, someone succeeds in growing it in zone 5.

A number of conifers are not listed. Either they are not suitable for the general climate conditions of the United States or they are too rare to be listed in any reliable source, or they are so esoteric as to lie beyond the garden pale.

I've listed the conifers alphabetically by genus, and I use their botanical species name, not the common name. The *Taxus* species—or yews—are listed separately, since they do not bear true cones.

They are: *Abies,* the firs; *Cedrus,* the cedars; *Chamaecyparis,* the false cypress; *Cryptomeria,* the Japanese cedar; *Juniperus,* the juniper; *Picea,* the spruce; *Pinus,* the pine; *Pseudotsuga,* the Douglas fir; *Sequoia,* the redwood; *Thuja,* the arborvitae; and *Tsuga,* the hemlock.

My code is as follows: UH means ultimate height, US means ultimate spread, and AGR means the annual growth rate.

FIRS AND THEIR CULTIVARS

Abies. The firs are members of the pine family and represent some forty species of the genus *Abies* (a'-bees). They are cone-bearing trees that are evergreen and monoecious, (which means they have both the male and female flowers on the same plant); they are usually found in the cooler regions of the Northern Hemisphere. Generally they are pyramidal or conelike in silhouette, having tall, straight trunks without a great deal of forking; the lower branches tend to fall away with age, and some species can reach a height of over 300'.

Firs prefer good soil: they resent shallow and alkaline ground and do their best in areas of high rainfall and moist

45

Abies balsamea 'Nana'

Abies concolor 'Green Globe'

Abies amabilis 'Spreading Star'

earth. Because of this the smaller trees would benefit from a mulch, especially in areas that have long, hot, and dry summers. As a genus they dislike heavy pollution and so are not the best for city gardens. Pruning should be done in spring.

Fir leaves are flat on the upper side with a deep blue-green color; the underside is keeled, and a pale or off-white band is found on either side of the midrib. When winds blow the branches about, these pale bands contrast sharply with the green of the needle tops and are an attractive aspect of the tree.

Flowers appear in the spring with the male catkins on side shoots and the female flowers closer to the tip of the branch. Cones mature during the summer, changing color from violet, blue, green, or yellow to brown. They stand upright rather than hang and break up as soon as they are ripe, with the seeds and cone scales falling off the tree at the same time.

Cultivars are propagated by grafting a selected branch onto a seedling tree.

The Cultivars

Abies amabilis is known as the red silver fir and grows to a height of 200′ in the Pacific Northwest. The trunk is almost white in tone, and cones begin their growth with a purple cast. One small plant is found in cultivation, *A. amabilis* 'Spreading Star.' It is a prostrate form hardy to zone 5 with an AGR of 1″–2″. When left alone it will cover a fairly large area over the years, never topping 3′ in height.

Abies balsamea is the Balsam fir of North America. Wild trees grow to some 75′ in height and make excellent Christmas trees. When I attended biology labs in high school and college, the gum from these trees was used in the preparation of microscope slides, since it would securely hold a glass cover slip to the slide itself. Before the discovery of chicle, balsam sap was happily chewed. Two cultivars are:
A. balsamea 'Nana': a round bush hardy to zone 3 that eventually makes a diameter of 3′ with an AGR of 2″–3″.
A. balsamea 'Hudsoniana': a pygmy form originally discovered in the White Mountains of New Hampshire with a UH of 2′–3′, a US of 2′–3′, and an AGR of 2″–3″.

Abies concolor, or the white fir, is found in the Southwest, where it is hardy to zone 4 and grows about 200' high. The bark is gray and the cones are purplish before maturity. This is one of the few firs that will tolerate some heat and dryness. Two cultivars are:

A. concolor 'Green Globe': found growing in a cemetery in New Jersey. It is hardy to adverse city conditions, making a round ball of sagegreen needles. The UH is 5'-8', US is 6'-9', and AGR is 3"-6".

A. concolor 'Candicans': has been justly called one of the most beautiful of blues found in the conifer clan. The upper leaves are silvery blue and the tree itself forms a cone. AGR is 6", and in forty years the tree is expected to be but 20' high. It is said that only strong terminal shoots can be used for propagation, since the side shoots will form a tree that lacks the desired cone shape. Mine seems to be spreading out more than it should, but the color is so fine that it makes scant difference to me.

Abies concolor

Abies koreana or the Korean fir is hardy to zone 5, grows to some 50' in nature, and hails from two isolated mountain areas in Korea. Cones are a violet-purple and are produced by fairly young trees. Spring needles are a silver-gray that contrasts sharply with the dark green of mature leaves. A mature tree will be about 30' high with an AGR of 8". Thus even a species is a fine choice for the small garden. Two cultivars are:

A. koreana 'Prostrata' will only reach 5' to 6' when mature with a US of 6'-8' and an AGR of 5"-6". If a leader develops, it must be cut away to keep the plant growing low to the ground.

A. koreana 'Compact Dwarf' is very, very slow, forming a compact bun with an AGR of 1"-2". This form does not bear cones.

Korean fir
Abies Koreana

Abies lasiocarpa, or the alpine fir, grows to 100' high in the mountains of the American West. The needles are a dark blue-green with a silver white bloom on the upperside, and the trunk is ashen gray. The cones are a beautiful purple.

A. lasiocarpa var. *arizonica* is called the Arizona cork bark fir and has produced one cultivar now termed *A. l.* 'Compacta.' This is a perfect fir tree that is pyramidal in habit but small in stature, with the typical blue-silver needles but never growing taller than 4'-6'. The US at the base is 3'-4' and the AGR is 3"-4".

49

THE CEDARS AND THEIR CULTIVARS

Cedrus. The cedars are Old World members of the pine family and belong to the genus *Cedrus* (sed'-rus). Often confused with the arborvitae and the junipers of the Americas, true cedars grow wild only in the Mediterranean region and the Himalayas. Though beautiful, they are only reliably hardy to zone 6 and then only with protection from bitter winds.

There are only four species of these evergreen trees. Bark color is gray and trunks become tall and massive with age, with older trees becoming the quintessential statement of stark beauty.

Flowers appear in the middle of summer and cones take two to three years to ripen and usually fall apart after releasing the seeds.

Cultivars are grafted for propagation, and the trees require a fairly well drained soil with a slightly acid pH, though some will tolerate a touch of alkalai in the soil.

The Cultivars

Cedrus atlantica, or the Atlantic cedar, grows to 20' or more in the Atlas Mountains of North Africa. Three outstanding cultivars are:

C. atlantica 'Glauca,' or the blue atlas cedar, has blue-green needles and blue cones. It grows to about 14' in ten years with a general pyramidal shape. Branches start to hang down as the tree matures, and within some fifty years the diameter at base will be some 25' to 30'.

C. atlantica 'Glauca Pendula' is the weeping blue cedar and one of those trees that frustrates those of us who live in areas of the country with winters too severe for the cedar. It must be raised as a standard or grafted onto a standard in order to prevent the foliage from growing flat upon the ground. Most nurseries stock it as a 4'–5' tree, and it will eventually need as much growing room as the 'Glauca.' If you have the room and climate, seek this splendid tree out!

C. atlantica 'Pendula' has green leaves rather than blue and is a weeping form best suited for the rock garden. It is a slow grower, making 3' of height in twenty years with an AGR of 2". It is a perfect form for planting on the edge of a rock bank so that the branches eventually will drape over the edge.

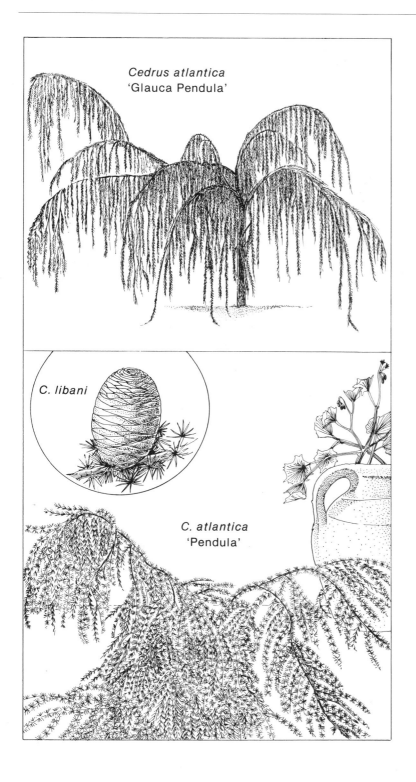

Cedrus atlantica 'Glauca Pendula'

C. libani

C. atlantica 'Pendula'

51

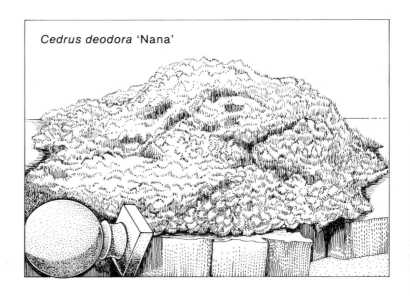

Cedrus deodora 'Nana'

Cedrus deodara, the Himalayan cedar, has longer leaves—up to 2″—than others in the clan of a blue-green tone. In nature the trees can top 150′, but in the garden many years are required to reach such a height. Two cultivars are available:

    C. deodara 'Aurea' is a much smaller tree than the wild species, with an AGR of 6″ and a UH of some 16′. The golden color is more pronounced where the leaves are exposed to sun and weather. The greatest glow appears in the spring. The growth is pyramidal, but unfortunately this tree is only hardy to zone 7 and even then needs some protected spot.

    C. deodara 'Nana' is hardy to zone 6 probably because it hugs the ground and is easier to protect from the winter winds. AGR is less than ½″, and this conifer never grows more than a few inches high.

Cedrus libani is the famous cedar of Lebanon often mentioned in the Bible. With a penchant to grow upwards of 100′ and live on for hundreds of years, the species is not exactly suited to the suburban garden.

    C. libani 'Nana' is hardy to zone 6 and a slow-growing bush of compact habit. It should grow no higher than 5′ in fifty years, with an AGR of 1″. Like *C. deodara* 'Nana,' this is a cultivar to experiment with in areas colder than zone 6, since its ground-hugging potential makes it easier to protect from winter chills.

THE FALSE CYPRESS

Chamaecyparis (kam-ee-sip'-are-is). The false cypress are evergreen trees with aromatic foliage that are often combined in botanical nomenclature with the *Cupressus,* or true cedars, but differ in having flatter branches and smaller cones that mature in the first season. The generally monoecious species forms are pyramidal in growth habit, occasionally tending to the columnar. Of the seven species, five have produced many cultivars and number among the most popular evergreens for the garden. Typical conifer flowers appear in the spring and the cones are small, round, and brown.

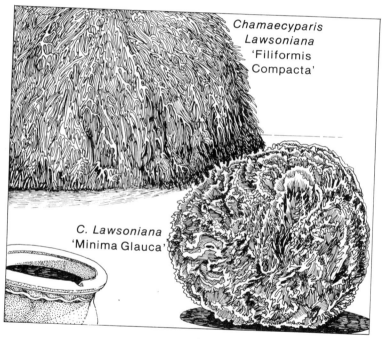

Chamaecyparis Lawsoniana 'Filiformis Compacta'

C. Lawsoniana 'Minima Glauca'

These trees do best in a slightly acid soil (pH 6.5) and should be kept moist but well drained. Although a fairly hardy tree, older and more exposed specimens can easily windburn in severe winters, so protection should be considered. Though they will tolerate some shade, full exposure to sun is needed to bring out colors in the foliage.

Pruning should be done in the spring, but generally these trees look best if just left to grow in their own way.

The Cultivars

Chamaecyparis lawsoniana, or Lawson's cypress, grows to 100' or more in the Pacific Northwest, where it is an extremely valuable timber tree. Though the species tree makes a valuable windbreak or lawn specimen, it is generally too large for the average lot or garden. Three fine cultivars are available:

C. lawsoniana 'Filiformis Compacta' will form a 3'-high bun and about the same width in ten years' time. The foliage has threadlike sprays of a blue-green hue with an AGR of 3″. Perched on a bank, this plant will be a fine accent in a small rock garden or evergreen planting. While hardy in zone 6, my tree lasted two years but perished when − 20° winds zapped it here in zone 5 during the cold winter of '77.

C. lawsoniana 'Minima Aurea' grows as a bright golden ball that slowly becomes a cone-shaped shrub over the years. With an AGR of 1¼″, it requires some ten years to produce a plant about 20″ high and 15″ wide at the base. The color turns to more of a green as the year's foliage matures. This plant still lives in my mountain garden but hugs a fern-covered bank with the house a scant 10' distant.

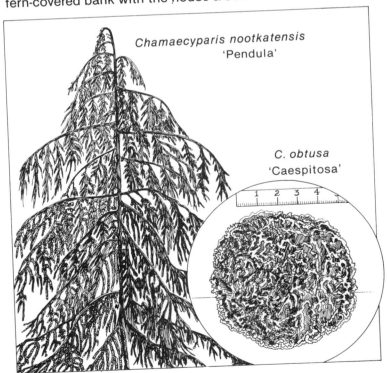

Chamaecyparis nootkatensis 'Pendula'

C. obtusa 'Caespitosa'

C. lawsoniana 'Minima' has green fan-shaped foliage with an AGR of 1¼ ". It forms a round ball with a 24" diameter after ten years of growth and can best be described as charming. It too needs protection, and deep snow—this problem will be continually mentioned with small trees—can severely damage and break the branches of this tiny tree, merely by slight packing. Never plant this or others like it under overhanging eaves or near drive and walkways where shoveled or plowed snow will eventually destroy it.

Chamaecyparis nootkatensis is the Nootka cypress or Alaska cedar, a tree that grows to 100' or more in the wild and

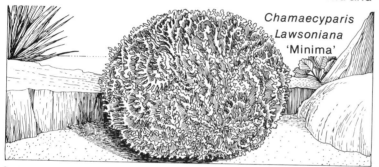

Chamaecyparis Lawsoniana 'Minima'

is a most valuable timber tree. Cones are small and round and the bark is ashen brown. Trees are on record that are over 275 years old. Even though it's from Alaska, this tree still needs some protection from severe winter winds; in nature it grows along the coast and the islands of southeastern Alaska and British Columbia, where winters are not as bad as they are in the mountains of New York. Two fine cultivars are offered:

C. nootkatensis 'Glauca Compacta' grows as an oval when young with glaucous foliage that twists to one side in growth. After some twenty years, a tree should be about 5' high and the same in width at the widest diameter.

C. nootkatensis 'Pendula,' or the weeping Alaska cedar, is a top-notch beauty that will reach some 33' in the same number of years. At the age of ten years it should average 10' in height and some 3' wide at its widest part. Unlike many evergreens, this particular tree can withstand wet feet and makes a fine pool or pondside specimen. The weeping character is more pronounced and is especially beautiful when reflected in a pool of water. If your climate will support this tree, it is one to consider for the garden.

Chamaecyparis obtusa is known as the Hinoki cypress and originally hails from Japan, where it is one of the major members of the timber industry. It will grow to over 100′ in nature. Some thirty cultivars are listed in reference books, and most of them have originated in Japan as direct results of their interest in dwarf and bonsai specimens. The foliage is easily identified by white lines that resemble stick figures on the undersides. Most of these cultivars are hardy to zone 5.

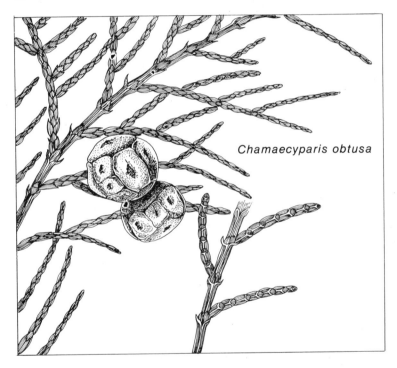

Chamaecyparis obtusa

    C. obtusa 'Caespitosa': This miniature tree is quite worthy of the epithet "cute." It is one of the smaller evergreens available, and if you are limited in growing space, 'Caespitosa' is perfect. A ten-year-old tree will barely top 3″ in height by 4″ in diameter. Since it is so easily damaged by compacting snow, winds, or hail, the best way to grow this plant is in a pot, bringing it inside for winter protection. One note of caution: This doesn't mean into a heated room. In order to survive, this tree—like all others from a changing climate—must go into dormancy during the winter months at a temperature no higher than 40°F. Either that or bury the pot in the earth and mulch extremely well or store the plant in a cold frame from December to March. This tree looks for all the world like the results of crocheting with green and yellow thread.

C. obtusa 'Coralliformis' is prostrate in habit with twisting threadlike stems that give it the look of its namesake, coral. It should form a bush of some 30″ in height with a like width after ten years of growth. Records say that after twenty-five years it will be only 5′ high.

C. obtusa 'Crippsii' is termed the golden Hinoki cypress, for the foliage is golden during three seasons of the year, fading a little in winter. Growth form is a broad pyramid with branches that sweep up only to dip at the ends. AGR is 6″–8″ and it should reach a height of 10′–12′ in ten years. UH should be 25′.

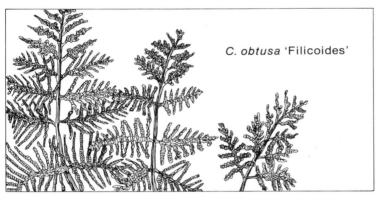

C. obtusa 'Filicoides'

C. obtusa 'Filicoides' is termed the fernspray cypress, and unlike the others of this genus, it seems to be able to withstand more cold and is successfully grown in zone 4. The foliage is moss green and grows in flattened sprays that tend to be untidy, with some branches growing out more than others. This can be remedied by pruning in the spring. If left alone it becomes a spreading bush. AGR is 6″ with UH some 6′–8′ and the majority of growth occurring in the first ten years.

C. obtusa 'Kosteri' forms fans of foliage that look as though they were mounting the DNA spiral or forming a small spiral staircase. If ever a tree looked as though it had a built-in Japanese gardener, this is it. AGR is 8″–10″ but should only reach a height of 30″ with 30″ at the base after ten years of growth. There is a tendency for this plant to sprawl but by pruning the side leaders, it will go up rather than out. It should be hardy in zone 4 if planted in a protected space.

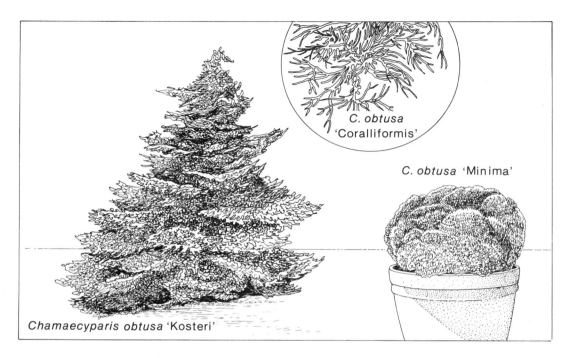

C. obtusa 'Coralliformis'

C. obtusa 'Minima'

Chamaecyparis obtusa 'Kosteri'

C. obtusa 'Juniperoides' is another candidate for either a sheltered spot in the rock garden or a pot to be taken in during the winter. A true miniature, it is sometimes called the tennis ball cypress. This small affair will fill out 6″ for each ten years of growth. The color is rich green.

C. obtusa 'Lycopodioides' is termed the clubmoss cypress, since its foliage grows as whiplike threads of green that turn in all directions. It forms an open bush; with an AGR of 6″ it gradually reaches some 6′ in height and 6′–8′ in width after thirty years of effort. Lycopodia is the genus name for the clubmosses; the resemblance is striking.

C. obtusa 'Nana' is one of the oldest evergreens in continual cultivation. The Japanese have been using it in rock and stone gardens for centuries, and the British for well over a hundred years. Its foliage is dark green and forms small cups that grow in tiers on the stubby stems. After some thirty years it will be 30″ high and 30″ wide in a rough oval. The perennial snow problem threatens this form, and it's best protected or potted up and taken indoors.

C. obtusa 'Nana Gracillis' grows slowly to a height of 2′. With the best growing conditions it may make 5′ of growth in thirty-some years with a US of 3′. The shape is a pyramid of dark green foliage with a lighter green edge.

C. obtusa 'Tetragona Aurea': I had to take a quick trip to the back garden to refresh my memory before describing this particular tree. It's a rugged little plant with bright yellow tips—so bright that it gleams like gold in the morning sun. I planted it against a bank to provide a bit of shelter from our sub-zero mountain winds, but with a background of shaded green it seems to be even more attractive than usual. AGR is 6″–8″ and its pyramid of stabbing growth should reach a height of 6′–8′ in ten years. This particular specimen is a must in any garden or group of evergreens for shape, habit, and glowing color.

Chamaecyparis pisifera—in Japan the Sawara cypress—is another Japanese tree capable of reaching over 100′ in its native country but has been the source of some thirty garden cultivars. Like all the others in this genus, some protection is needed in the worst parts of zone 5.

These particular trees often exhibit three different types of foliage: juvenile, which is soft and feathery to the touch and termed 'squarrosa'; intermediate, which is a compromise between soft and prickly and called 'plumosa'; and the adult form, which is sharp to the touch, 'pisifera.' There is a fourth or threadlike leaf termed 'filifera.'

C. pisifera 'Boulevard' was originally termed *Retinispora pisifera squarrosa cyano-viridis* when it was initially introduced to the world in 1934. That mouthful has been diminished over the years, but the plant is still one of the most popular. The color is a blue-gray. Growth is pyramidal in form, reaching a height of 6′ in ten years. AGR is 6″. It might grow to 20′ in thirty years.

C. pisifera 'Plumosa' is the intermediate type of Sawara cypress with soft-looking foliage that feels quite sharp to the touch when it has dried. The light-green foliage grows in an uneven cone, reaching a height of 10′ in ten years with a base growth of 3′.

C. pisifera 'Plumosa Aurea' exhibits new growth of golden yellow in the spring that later turns to the typical green. The UH is 25′ if left unchecked and unpruned. AGR is a healthy 8″ and leads to a tree about 10′ high and 6′ wide at the base in ten years' time. The gold turns to brown for the winter.

C. pisifera 'Aurea Nana' will only be 5′ high and 3′ wide at the base in ten years, but it retains the golden color throughout the entire year.

Chamaecyparis pisifera
'Filifera Aurea'

C. pisifera 'Plumosa Compressa' is the smallest form of the intermediate group of foliage and makes a round ball of yellow-green that turns brownish in winter. In ten years' time it makes a grand statement of 8″. This is another that does well potted for protection from the snow.

C. pisifera 'Filifera Aurea' grows very slowly and, as far as climate is concerned, is the exception that proves the rule. My plant is located on the top of a bank that bears the brunt of icy winds from the west. Every year I lose some foliage, but the tree itself continues to do well. The color is a bright yellow in summer that turns a golden brown in winter. The foliage is so dense that it is difficult to probe the interior. UH is 12′–16′ with a US of 5′–8′ and AGR of 8″. This is an extra-special plant and should find its way to most gardens.

C. pisifera 'Squarrosa' is the original plant with soft blue-green foliage that came from Japan in the middle 1800s. Depending on growing conditions, it might have a UH of between 15′–30′ if left unpruned. In ten years it will form a soft pyramid with a 10′-wide base and a height of 6′. The undersides of the foliage are silvery, and the gracefully weeping branch tips are especially beautiful.

C. pisifera 'Squarrosa minima' has an AGR of only 2″–3″ with foliage of a beautiful sea-green hue. UH is but 3′, forming a tight bun. Any leaders that develop should be sheared off to retain the compact growth.

C. pisifera 'Snow' is a new introduction at most nurseries that stock other *Chamaecyparis.* It is a Japanese introduction with the 'Squarrosa' type of foliage of a light gray-green, but the tips of the branches are dusted with white during the growing season. It should reach a height of 6′ in ten years. In addition to winter protection, it needs some shelter from the hot noon sun of July and August, or the tips will be burned.

A gardener who feels at sea with the seemingly unending variations on evergreens could do worse than specialize in the *Chamaecyparis* alone. While those listed represent the more common cultivars, a few of the sources listed in Chapter 5 carry some of the rarer forms and each year sees newer varieties on the plant market. Like a collector of one kind of jewel rather than a hodgepodge of many, these gems will more than pay back their initial investment in a few short years of growth.

THE JAPANESE CEDAR

Cryptomeria. The temple cedars of Japan, called *Cryptomeria* (crip-to-meer'-e-a), generally reach a height of 120′ in their native land and are used both for timber and working into ornaments. The wood is also intensely fragrant.

These trees require more warmth than the average evergreen and are not reliably hardy north of zone 7. Even then they need some protection from cold winds. In addition they need adequate water, so are poor choices for a hot and dry climate.

Soil should be well-drained and slightly on the acid side; if it's too heavy, some organic matter should be worked in before planting.

Male and female flowers appear on different parts of the same branches; the buds are produced in the fall and open the following spring, so all pruning must be done in late spring. Cones are brown when ripe and about ½ ″ in diameter. The leaves are light green, turning brown in winter.

The only species is *C. japonica* and some thirty cultivars are listed.

C. japonica 'Cristata' is an unusual form that produces fasciated growths on branch tips situated among normal foliage. These fan-shaped stems look like the cockscomb on a rooster. The AGR is 6″ with UH of 6′–8′, and it will form an irregular pyramid. This particular cultivar will endure zone 5 but will burn with sub-zero winds.

Cryptomeria japonica 'Cristata'

C. japonica 'Nana' grows as a small bush with weeping tips. It grows exceedingly slowly; it will form an oval 3′ high in twenty-five years. Foliage is light green.

C. japonica 'Vilmoriniana' forms a low mound of dark green in the growing season that turns brownish green in winter. Growth form is an oval-shaped bush of tightly packed foliage, with a ten-year-old being some 20″ high and 15″ wide.

THE JUNIPERS

Juniperus. The scientific name for the Juniper clan is *Juniperus* (jew-nip'-er-us), which represents about seventy species of evergreen trees and shrubs, all quite hardy in the northern reaches of the United States.

Though bonafide members of the pine family, junipers produce a berrylike fruit. But on close examination, this berry turns out to be a modified cone coated with resin, and dusted with a bloom, whose pungent perfume can readily be identified as a flavoring agent of gin.

Leaves have two forms: the juvenile are awl-like or needle-shaped, while the adult forms are scalelike, clasping the shoot and overlapping.

Soil demands are minimal: lightly acid to neutral pH; most even do well in calcareous soils. It needs watering during extended dry spells and should be pruned in spring, when any branches damaged in winter can be removed.

Juniper branch with berry-like cones.

Juniperus chinensis, or the Chinese juniper, can reach a height of 65' in its native lands of China, Mongolia, and Japan. The tree is upright and forms a broad cone or pyramid. The plants are dioecious—male and female flowers on separate trees—with only the females bearing conelike berries.

Although *Hortus III* describes over seventy cultivars, the following four are generally available in cultivation.

J. chinensis 'Iowa' is one of a number of introductions made by the late Professor T. J. Maney of Iowa State College. It is one of a number of junipers that make fine vertical accents in a general horizontal planting. The growth in ten years will be some 6' high with a basal diameter of 3'. The color is a fine blue-green.

63

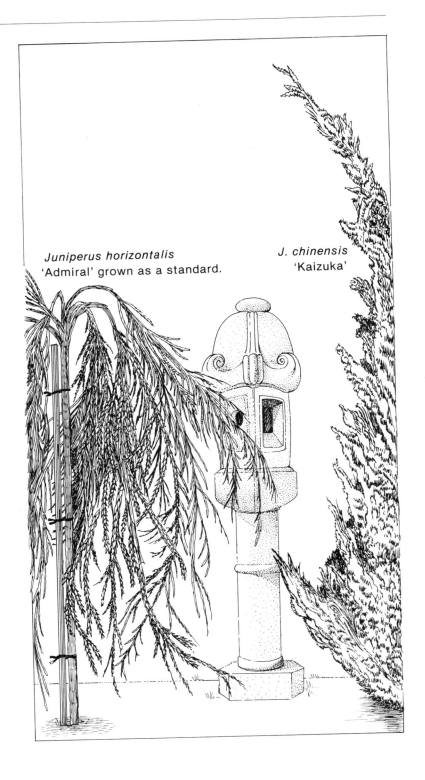

Juniperus horizontalis
'Admiral' grown as a standard.

J. chinensis
'Kaizuka'

J. chinensis 'Kaizuka' also bears the name in old catalogs of 'Torulosa' and is called the Hollywood juniper in popular parlance. The normal growth is upright, but the branches may be pruned with ease, allowing the bush to spread. It will grow some 10' in ten years with a bottom 4' in width. If left alone, the UH should be 25'. The color is a bright green. The tree will withstand vigors of climate: from the heat of southern California to the cold of Iowa. It is also resistant to the ravages of pollution.

J. chinensis 'Mountbatten' is hardy to the frigid grip of zone 3 since it originated as a mutant seedling in a Canadian nursery. If not pruned back, it will reach a UH of 16', attaining 10' of growth in ten years. Growth form is pyramidal.

J. chinensis 'Pyramidalis' grows as its cultivar name implies, in the shape of a pyramid with a UH of 16' and a base 5'–6' wide. Color is the typical blue-green and makes a very attractive specimen tree. The best adjective to describe it would be *neat.*

Juniperus communis is the common juniper, which varies from a low shrub to a 25' tree and grows along rocky hillsides and pastures in the cooler states of the Northwest to Northeast. The bark is thin and shreds with ease, and needles are sharp with a topside of blue-green and a gray-white underside. In windswept locations this small tree becomes most picturesque, many times hugging the ground. The berries turn from green to dark blue as they ripen. Three interesting cultivars are usually available.

J. communis 'Compressa' grows as a perfect little column that will top 10" after ten years of growth. Its color is dark green and the foliage is so tightly packed that this little tree looks almost solid. A grouping of these on a bank of hillside rockgarden would be striking indeed. Zone 4.

J. communis 'Echiniformis' gets its name from a supposed resemblance to a sea urchin but looks—in profile—exactly like a European hedgehog. This bun-shaped bush grows slowly to reach a diameter of 12" in ten years and a height of 6". Color is light green.

J. Communis 'Depressa Aurea' is a carpet juniper of a beautiful yellow-bronze that darkens to green with the approach of winter. While reaching a spread of 4' in ten years it should rarely exceed 12" in height and can then be pruned to keep within wanted bounds.

65

Juniperus horizontalis is a prostrate and trailing shrub that is found growing on dry and barren soil from Newfoundland south to New York and west to Minnesota. They have given rise to some thirty named cultivars, the most common of which are quickly planted on the barren slopes of new gas stations and hamburger stands in an effort to disguise what lies within. The following six are generally available:

J. horizontalis 'Admirabilis' holds its main branches flat against the ground while the side branches swing up and away into the air. The color is a rich gray-green, and it can spread to a circle of 10′ in diameter in ten years. Leading branches can be pruned for the first few years to make the new growth more bushy.

J. horizontalis 'Bar Harbor' originally came from Mount Desert Island in Maine and shares the growth habit of 'Admirabilis,' with the main branches following the contours of ground or rock. It is usually gray-green during the growing season but turns to a fine mauve-purple during the winter months. AGR is 15″, and over years a sizable area of ground can be covered.

J. horizontalis 'Blue Chip' assumes the growth habits of the most of the others in this group, but the color is a pronounced blue that is held by the foliage throughout the year.

J. horizontalis 'Douglasii' originated 125 years ago in Waukegan, Illinois, and carries the popular name of the Waukegan juniper. With an AGR of some 15″, this plant is another one of the fine ground covers available. The main branches hug the ground and the side shoots swerve upward. The color is blue-green during the growing season and purple-blue in the winter. 'Douglasii' makes a fine choice for gardeners who must work with extremely sandy soil and does quite well in a seaside planting.

J. horizontalis 'Glomerata' has a much slower AGR (4″) and makes a small mat of 6″-high light-green foliage, changing to the species purple for the winter. When compared with the others of this group, 'Glomerata' can best be termed a dwarf.

J. horizontalis 'Wiltonii' is silver-blue in color and truly hugs the ground as it grows its AGR of 9″. Since its height rarely goes above 6″, its common names of Blue Rug or Carpet Juniper are most apt. This particular cultivar is often offered in nursery and garden centers.

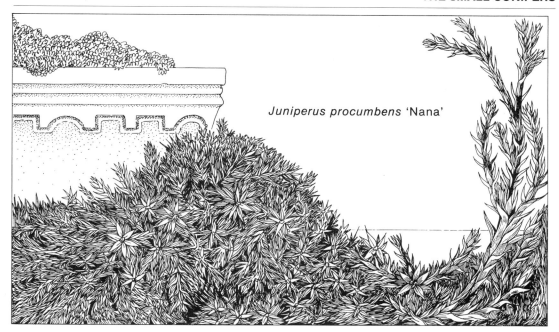

Juniperus procumbens 'Nana'

I must pause and note again that the previous plants are the almost perfect solution for covering second-rate soil (and a poor exposure) with first-rate garden growth. They all transplant with ease, require the minimum of upkeep, endure dry seasons and winter winds, yet will respond with a fine crop of new and expanding growth every spring.

Juniperus procumbens is a Japanese ornamental discovered in the mountains of Japan some hundred years ago. It was considered a botanical treasure when found and is still going strong today. AGR is 6″, and in time one plant will fill a circle of 25′ diameter. One cultivar is offered by most suppliers and its color and growth habit make it a must.

J. procumbens 'Nana' has an AGR of 4″–6″ and is called the dwarf Japanese juniper. The foliage is a fresh green in spring, turning to a blue-green with summer's advance, and ending as bronzed for the winter. It was introduced to America by the Hill Nursery of Dundee, Illinois, in 1904 as *J. japonica nana* until receiving its new name in 1942.

This plant will eventually cover an area diameter of 10′–12′. Of all the ground huggers, this particular tree is my favorite. The needles are sharp, so sharp that it came as a surprise to me when I found that deer—when pressed by hunger—will devour this creeper, patiently removing needle after needle and leaving naked bark.

67

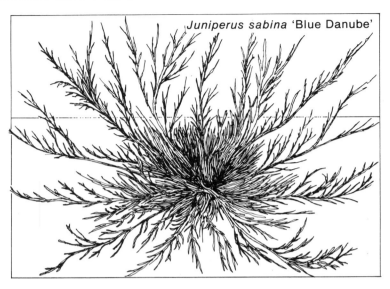

Juniperus sabina 'Blue Danube'

Juniperus sabina, or the savin juniper, is a shrub growing to some 10' in height that comes from the mountains of Europe and Asia. They are extremely hardy—facing zone 3 without a shiver—and two cultivars are particularly useful as ground covers.

J. sabina 'Blue Danube' originally hails from Austria and forms a low shrub of a silver blue-green. Main branches hug the ground, while the side branches turn up at an angle. It will cover a diameter of 4' in ten years, staying at the species height level.

J. sabina 'Tamariscifolia,' or the tamarix juniper, is a similar cultivar that is still found in the wilds of southern Europe so is often found in some listings as *J. sabina* var. *tamariscifolia.* It forms a compact mound of very prickly green foliage that will cover an area 4' in diameter in ten years and grow to a height of some 20".

Juniperus scopulorum is known as the Rocky Mountain red cedar and is quite hardy to zone 4. In nature it's found some 5,000' above sea level and is considered by some to be a subspecies of *Juniperus virginiana.* One cultivar is now available, called 'Blue Heaven.' The silver-blue of the foliage is truly beautiful, and it will grow straight up to 6' in ten years, being some 20" wide at the base. This is another fine tree for a vertical accent, and even young plants are often covered with berries. I put my specimen near a Japanese red maple and the colors glow together.

Over one hundred years ago, a large number of hybrids were developed between *Juniperus chinensis* and *Juniperus sabina.* They are now termed *Juniperus × media* with the best-known member of the cross being the bane of every foundation planting in the Northeast, the Pfitzer, or *Juniperus × media* 'Pfitzeriana.' Well can I remember being asked by my mother to get the weeds that would on occasion grow beneath those sweeping boughs: It was a prickly job.

The problem with the Pfitzer is that it gets quite large. At fifteen years one plant may be 9' wide and 4' high. What started as a small plant to cover a concrete basement wall soon overpowers all else. But for a quick landscape fix, these are still outstanding trees.

J. × media 'Pfitzeriana Compacta', or Nick's compact juniper, is a shorter version of the general type that only grows 3' high by 3' wide in ten years.

J. media 'Pfitzeriana Glauca' has the same general form as the standard Pfitzer, but it is a lovely shade of silver-blue that turns to a purple-brown during the winter.

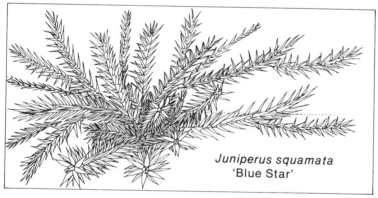

Juniperus squamata
'Blue Star'

Juniper squamata tends to be a shrub from the mountains of southeast Asia and quite hardy to zone 5. Some twelve cultivars are listed, but the following three represent the best of the species.

J. squamata 'Loderi' forms a conical tree that stands erect and reaches a height of some 4' in ten years.

J. squamata 'Blue Star' is a recent introduction from Holland, notable for its dense growth, its steel-blue foliage that truly resembles the twinkling of stars, and the spreading habit of growth. The UH is 3'–4' and the US is 5'. This plant promises to be a horticultural star, with everyone rushing to plant it. That's not all bad, since it is a beauty.

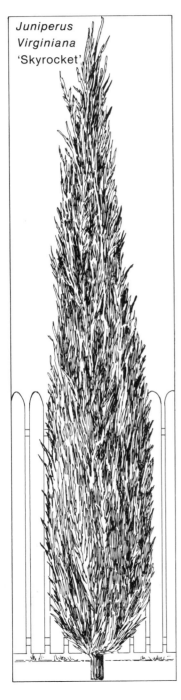

Juniperus
Virginiana
'Skyrocket'

J. squamata 'Wilsoni' is slower growing, with the average making only a spreading bush of 4' high and 4' wide in ten years. The foliage is a light gray-green. There are two white bands on the inner sides of each leaf and when viewed in certain light and weather conditions, these bands impart a wonderful silvery effect.

Juniperus × media
'Pfitzeriana'

Juniperus virginiana is an American tree that grows between 40' and 50' high in the wilds and produces the wood that is used for cedar chests, fenceposts, and pencil wood. It thrives in zone 3, and the only problem it presents is its role as alternate host for apple rust: if your garden is in close proximity to a working apple orchard, this tree is not for you. A number of cultivars are offered, but one is outstanding:

J. virginiana 'Skyrocket' is more than aptly named. This is one of the only upright, narrow-growing conifers—if not *the* only one—available today suitable to most climate conditions. It was originally found growing wild in the eastern United States, and happily someone found it in 1949. In ten years it will be 6'–8' tall with a UH of 25' but will only be 1' wide at the base. Color is silvery blue-green and as a vertical accent there is none other to compare. Some authorities list it as *J. scopulorum* 'Skyrocket,' but with either name it is not to be overlooked as a fine and welcome addition to any garden of evergreens.

THE SPRUCE AND THEIR CULTIVARS

Picea (pie'-see-a or PIC-ea) are well known evergreens that grow in a pyramidal or conical aspect much in use as Christmas trees. This genus includes the Norway spruce (*P. abies*), which is reputed to be the most widely planted evergreen tree in America.

The sharp needles are held to the branches by a tiny stem—called a *sterigma,* meaning prop—so when needles fall, the branch remains rough to the touch.

Typical conifer flowers bloom in the spring, with both male and female on the same branch, and the resultant cones are blue or green when young but ripen to brown and hang down from the branch. They remain on the trees after the ripe seeds have flown.

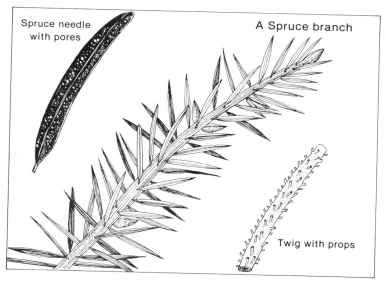

Spruce needle with pores

A Spruce branch

Twig with props

The spruces as a family are more tolerant to smoke and other urban pollutants and will do well in a wide variety of soil conditions, though they prefer a mildly acid balance. Prune any time of the garden year except when growth occurs in the spring. Be sure to leave a few growth buds on each stem.

The popular phrase *spruced up* is derived from the neat and orderly appearance of these trees.

Picea abies, the Norway spruce, tops 150′ in its native land and has been widely planted in the United States as an

71

ornamental—though it eventually outgrows its welcome—and a windbreak. The bark is rough and brown, and the cones fall after the first winter on the tree. At one time there were over 130 cultivars on nursery listings. We mention four.

P. abies 'Little Gem': The name is self explanatory as it truly is. It is a slow-growing dwarf form developed from a witches' broom that appeared on another cultivar, 'Nidiformis.' AGR is no more than 1″, and the US should be under 20″. The shape is round.

P. abies 'Nidiformis' is the popular bird's nest spruce, so called because young plants exhibit á slight depression in the top of center that closely resembles its namesake. Hardy to zone 3, it grows into a dense, flat-topped shrub with an AGR of 3″–4″ and a final diameter of about 6′ with a height of 4′–5′. The new buds in spring are a light and fine green that sparkles against the background of the mature and darker green needles.

P. abies 'Pygmaea,' or the pygmy spruce, is probably one of the earliest dwarf forms taken up by gardeners and nursery men. It was first offered in the mid-1800s. Its form is round with an AGR of 2″; it makes a globe about 1′ in diameter after ten years. After this hectic beginning, it then slows its growth by one-third. The needles are dark-green.

P. abies 'Repens' is known as the creeping spruce, but with an AGR of 1″ there are slim chances of its creeping too far. It will make a cushion-shaped mound not more than 20″ wide and 8″–10″ high after ten years.

Picea brewerana. Most of the evergreens mentioned in this book will rarely exceed 16′–20′ in height and then take some years to do so. The following tree is an exception: In some forty years, it should be about 30′ high. Why mention it? Sheer beauty. In nature it might grow to more than 100′, in the Siskiyou Mountains on the California–Oregon border.

It is perfectly hardy to zone 6, where its broad pyramid of drooping branches becomes the quintessence of all aspects of the brooding and romantic landscape; it can turn a suburban yard into a bit of Transylvania and the *Sorrows of Young Werther.*

Though it's not recommended for mass plantings as a specimen, this tree would be the talk of the neighborhood. There are, to my knowledge, no cultivars, but frankly none are needed.

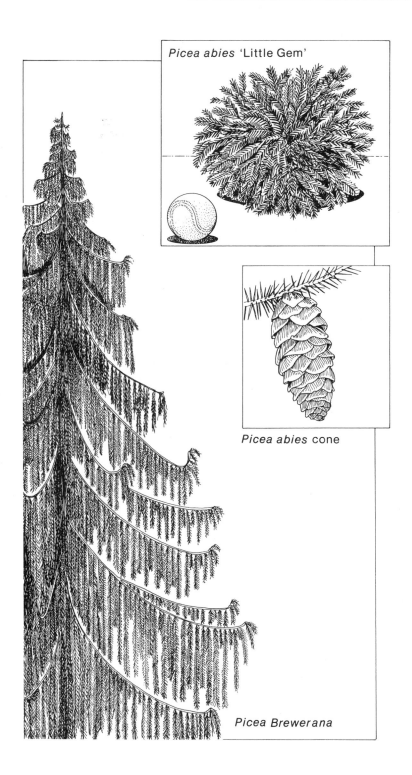

Picea abies 'Little Gem'

Picea abies cone

Picea Brewerana

Picea glauca is the famous white spruce that is a native of northern United States and Canada, where in the wild state it may reach 100′. The needles are blue-green. Two cultivars are generally available.

P. glauca 'Conica' is also called the dwarf Alberta spruce, since it was found in the wilds of Alberta in 1904 and has gone on to become one of the most popular dwarf evergreens in cultivation. Hardy to zone 3, the grass-green needles are so tightly packed that the tree looks like one solid mass. The UH should be some 15′, but it can be pruned in the spring to keep it from growing too large. AGR is 4″–6″ and it makes an almost perfect cone. I have a small specimen in the back garden that measures 18″ in height. It never fails to elicit comment since it's difficult to believe that anything in nature could look so perfect.

P. glauca 'Echiniformis' is a true dwarf among evergreens, with an AGR of only 1″–2″. The original appeared in France during the mid-1800s, and it has been popular ever since. the UH is only 30″, with a spread of some 3′. In growth it forms a small pin cushion of glaucous gray-green needles.

P. glauca 'Echiniformis'

Picea glauca 'Conica'

Picea mariana is the black spruce, which will grow up to 90′ high with a straight trunk and dark-green needles with a whitish bloom. Since it is one source of timber for construction, it is not quite right for the small backyard, but one cultivar is.

P. mariana 'Nana' makes a slow-growing mound of crowded needles of a light blue-green. At ten years it is only 8″ high and 10″ wide. The cones are a dark purple and are said to remain on the tree for some thirty years after the seeds are ripe.

Picea pungens 'Glauca Pendula'

Picea pungens is the Colorado spruce, which tops 100′ in nature—much too big for the average landscape. It is hardy to zone 3. There are a number of cultivars available with the fine blue foliage and slow growth.

P. pungens 'Globosa' is a slow-growing form with intense gray-blue needles. In ten years it will form a mound some 18″ high and 24″ wide.

P. pungens 'Glauca Pendula' is the weeping form of the Colorado spruce, with an AGR of 10″ and a UH of 8″–10″ if it is grown as a prostrate form by removing all upright leaders that appear. Its UH is 10′ if the leaders are allowed to develop. This tree is perfect to plant at the edge of a rock bank so that it may eventually hang over the edge for great effect.

75

THE PINES AND THEIR CULTIVARS

Pinus (pie'-nus), or the pine, is an evergreen and monoecious tree that represents some ninety species in the Northern Hemisphere and is the most valuable of all the timber trees. In fact, this magnificent tree produces most of today's building lumber, turpentine, and tar.

The needles are long, green, and graceful, growing in bundles of two, three, or five. Flowers bloom in the spring with male and female on the same branch. Cones are usually large and woody, some maturing the first year, in some species the second, and a few in the third year after the flowers bloom and pollenate.

Umbrella pine
Pinus densiflora
'Umbraculifera'

They prefer a position in full sun, but they can manage in some shade. They will tolerate all kinds of poor soil—even mostly rock—but resent continually wet feet; the one problem with a thin layer of poor soil is the eventual chance that a mature tree will topple in a wind storm, since its root system is too shallow for support.

Pruning consists of cutting the candles (new growth) in the late spring, but never remove it all. As a genus pines are all remarkably hardy and always picturesque.

Propagation of cultivars and rare varieties is by grafting the desired cutting onto a seedling tree that is closely related.

Five species are covered.

Pinus densiflora is a Japanese arrangement at any stage in its growth. While reaching a height of 100' in Japan, it will usually grow about 10' in ten years when planted out in your garden. With its tendency to bend its stems and the beautiful shade of red that colors the young bark, all in combination with the long and graceful needles, this is an oriental painting come to life. It can be held back in its growth with judicious pruning every spring and is hardy to zone 4 if protected from severe winter winds. Three fine cultivars are available.

P. densiflora 'Pendula,' or the weeping Japanese pine, usually grows as a small shrub with drooping branches that cascade with a marvelous effect over rock edges or trail along the ground. Some nurseries offer it after they have trained it upward on a small trunk, giving it more of a weeping effect. AGR is some 2", and a ten-year specimen would only measure 4' across.

Pinus densiflora 'Oculis-draconis'

P. densiflora 'Oculis-draconis' is called the dragon-eye pine and follows the growth pattern of the species with one difference: each and every needle is banded with a stripe of yellow. This is a particularly fine tree for a small garden.

P. densiflora 'Umbraculifera' is sometimes offered in the trade as *Pinus tanyosho,* but the first term is correct. This is a slow-growing cultivar, often termed the umbrella pine because the branches grow up and around from a central trunk like the ribs in a wind-turned umbrella. After thirty-five years it might reach a height of 15', and even if one didn't know that it came from Japan, one would immediately make that assumption. Like the others, this is hardy to zone 4. And if garden room is available, all three of the forementioned trees deserve a place of honor.

77

Pinus mugo, also known as the Swiss mountain pine, flourishes in zone 4 and will adapt to zone 3 with some protection. The average tree is a bun-shape and very slow to mature—though some trees in nature can reach a height of 30'. The needles are a rich and dark green, with the season's new growth so light as to be almost white. These trees are slightly tolerant to lime. Two cultivars are available.

P. mugo var. *mughus* forms a many-branched tree that reaches a height of 6' after some fifteen years of growth. This is the variety often termed the mugho pine in the trade. The growth habit of this tree reminds one of windswept moun-

Dwarf mountain pine
Pinus mugo

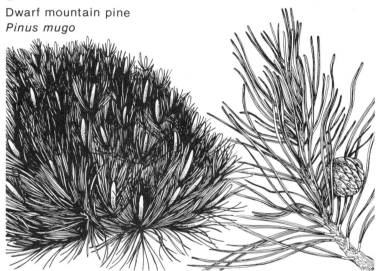

tains; it seems to fight against the forces of nature even when these climatic events are lacking.

P. mugo var. *pumilio* is the dwarf Swiss mountain pine and forms a bushy globe of a 5' diameter after enduring for thirty years in the garden. When planted in groups of three or five they are especially fine accents.

Pinus pumila is the Japanese stone pine. Sometimes called the Dwarf Siberian pine, its branches have a crowded look, since it holds its needles for three years before they drop. The needle color is blue-green and it is hardy in zone 4. It rarely exceeds 10'–12' in height with a ten-year-old inching in at 2'. Small violet-purple cones change to a red-brown as they mature.

P. pumila 'Glauca' is smaller than the parent just mentioned and has needles of a blue-gray shade.

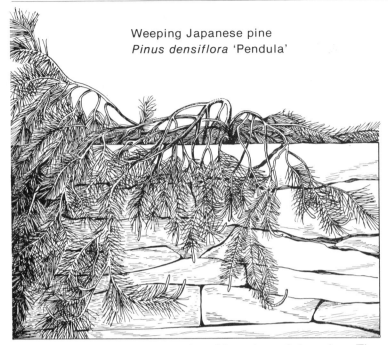

Weeping Japanese pine
Pinus densiflora 'Pendula'

Pinus strobus is the majestic white pine of America. The straight trunks of virgin trees were once used to form the masts of sailing ships, since many grew to a height of 200′. Sadly, like many things in this world, these trees were raped for all their potential uses. The majority of houses built in the Northeast during the beginning years of this century were built with this American heritage. Thanks to vast efforts in reforestation during the thirties, the white pine seems once again to be on the ascendant.

The general trunk diameter of a single tree is between 2′ and 3′ but some trees with a 6′ width have been recorded. A major pest is the white pine weevil, which kills the leader of a healthy tree at a height between 6′ and 12′, thus causing the tree to send up two leaders and dividing the main trunk into two smaller and less valuable branches. (The same weevil will also attack spruces).

While the species white pine is much too tall for the average garden prospects, there are fine cultivars available.

P. strobus 'Nana' is the dwarf form and will grow into a dense clump of needles with an AGR of between 2″ and 4″. In fact, needles are so thickly bunched that the trunk is never seen. The UH will probably be 8′ with the same diameter. The 'Nana' is grown by grafting a branch from a known cultivar onto a seedling of a normal type.

79

P. strobus 'Contorta' develops twisted branches that bear densely packed, twisted needles. After forty years a specimen will be 18′ high.

P. strobus 'Prostrata' bears 5″ needles that droop on branches that ramble over the ground, never forming leaders. My specimen is but a few years old and looks from a distance like a green Pekinese dog. The AGR is 8″–12″, and over the years a tree can become quite large, covering an oval over 7′ in diameter.

P. strobus 'Pendula' is the weeping form of the white pine and with an AGR of 12″–16″ can assume a height of 12′–15′ with a slightly smaller spread. It can be held back by pruning the leaders in the spring.

P. strobus 'Umbraculifera' bears crowded branches covered with light-green needles about 3½ ″ long that droop. The growth form is a tall oval.

Pinus strobus 'Prostrata'

Pinus sylvestris is the Scotch pine, well known in England and often used—when young—as a Christmas tree in the United States. In nature these valuable timber trees reach a height of 100′. Two small and fascinating cultivars are generally available.

P. sylvestris 'Argentea Compacta' is a very compact form of the tree, with an AGR of 2″. It grows in the form of a low bush.

P. sylvestris 'Viridis Compacta' bears lighter-than-type green needles that are twisted and contorted. It's a slow growing bush that will reach a height of 6′ in fifteen years.

Pinus sylvestris
'Viridis Compacta'

THE DOUGLAS FIR

The *Pseudotsuga* (soo-do-soo'-ga) is the name given to seven species of evergreen trees native to western North America, China, and Japan. Trees are monoecious, generally pyramidal in shape, and prefer a slightly acid soil, though they are tolerant of some lime. They are poor trees to plant in shallow soil, since the root systems spread out rather than down and give weak support to mature trees. At one time there were fifty cultivars listed for the Douglas fir (*P. menziesii*), a valuable timber source that tops 300' in nature. Douglas was

Douglas fir
Pseudotsuga Menziesii

David Douglas, a Scottish botanist who came to America in the early 1800s on a journey of discovery. The following two are available:

P. menziesii 'Compacta' is a small tree hardy to zone 4 that carries dark green needles and exhibits an AGR of 2"–3". The branches fan out on the horizontal, keeping a height of 2'–3' and a US of 4'–6'.

P. menziesii 'Pendula' is the weeping Douglas fir. Only hardy to zone 6, this form creeps along the ground, flowing like a waterfall over the edges of rocks and banks. The AGR is 2"–4".

82

THE REDWOODS

Everyone is familiar with the giant redwoods of California. Unfortunately they are not primed to grow in the east, and without taking a trip to the West Coast, the average gardener will never see one. There is a substitute, though, for the sequoia (sa-qwo'-ya) species of commerce and tourism, and that is a cultivar.

    S. sempervirens 'Adpressa' can be kept to a dwarf size by removing its upright leaders. It you don't, it can reach a height of 10'–16' in the gardener's lifetime—certainly no threat to crowding. Like its big brother, it is only hardy to zone 7; cold winds burn the new growth. I have mine in a pot that sits in the sun from early spring to late fall. It is then removed to an attic room, where it receives plenty of light and temperatures that hover around 35°F. It's important to remember that when a tree is kept indoors for the winter months, it must have an occasional drink of water, since the soil is not fully frozen solid, and it must have a period of cold (40°F. will do) to insure a dormant period necessary to the continued health and life of the plant.

    As I write this section, I can glance outside and see this gem of a tree with its new growth almost white, sparkling against the darker green of the mature leaves.

    If you are lucky enough to have a climate that allows you to plant such a tree outdoors, if it does outgrow your chosen spot—in your lifetime—it can be cut back to the ground, and new sprouts will soon appear.

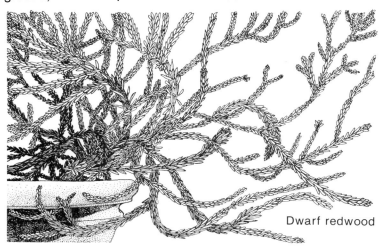

Dwarf redwood

83

THE ARBORVITAE

The arborvitaes, or *Thuja* (thoo'-ya), are native to North America and eastern Asia and comprise a family of trees valuable both for commerce and art. The name is a Latinized French term that means the Tree of Life, so termed by the members of Jacques Cartier's Canadian expedition, after they discovered that chewing the bark cured scurvy. It was also the first tree exported to Europe from the American colonies.

Trees are monoecious, with flowers at the tips of the branches and forming small brown cones. Growth is generally pyramidal. The trees prefer a slightly acid soil with decent drainage and some shelter from bitter winds.

Older trees will begin to spread—much like their gardener friends—and a general period of old age sets in after some thirty-five years. In some respects, this quality makes them easier to work with in today's society than their counterparts that live for 300 or 400 years.

Trees with yellow or golden foliage need a position with a goodly amount of full sun to develop their distinctive colorations.

Two spellings of the genus are found in listings: *Thuja* or *Thuya.* Both were names provided by Linnaeus on different dates; both are pronounced the same and both are thought to be correct. You take your pick.

Five species are listed botanically. Gardeners are generally concerned with *T. occidentalis* and *T. orientalis. T. orientalis* is now termed *Platycladus orientalis* in *Hortus III,* but since it will be years before all the nurseries change their catalogs to reflect the new term, I continue to use the old.

Thuja occidentalis is the American white cedar and grows to a 65' height in nature and is used commercially for poles, timbers, and shingles. An oil is also distilled from its leaves and used medicinally.

Over sixty cultivars have been listed over the years, pointing to the popularity of this fine tree. The following five are available:

T. occidentalis 'Ericoides' is termed the heath arborvitae because of the bronze-green tone of the foliage that turns to a deeper bronze in the winter. It is a globe-shaped plant,

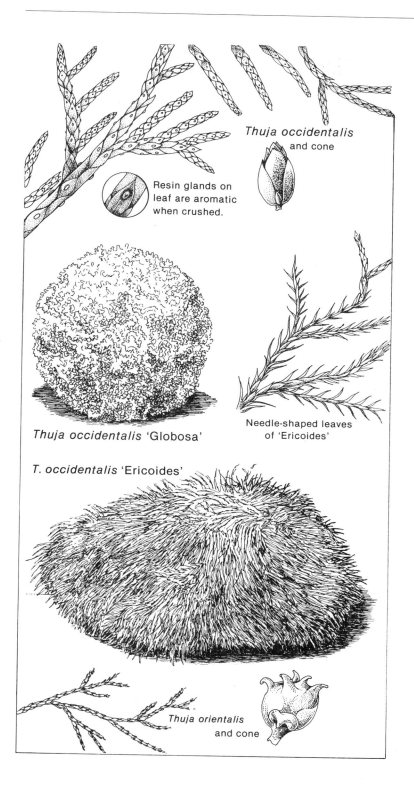

Thuja occidentalis and cone

Resin glands on leaf are aromatic when crushed.

Thuja occidentalis 'Globosa'

Needle-shaped leaves of 'Ericoides'

T. occidentalis 'Ericoides'

Thuja orientalis and cone

soft to the touch, with an AGR of 6″, making a specimen eight years old about 20″ high and 2′ wide.

T. occidentalis 'Globosa' is justly named since it forms a globe of light gray-green foliage that will reach a diameter of 4′ upon maturity. At ten years of age, it will be 3′ up and out.

T. occidentalis 'Hetz Midget' is used specifically for the rock garden or dwarf conifer bed, since it will only grow to a height of 2′ in some thirty years. After ten years it will be 12″ high. It is necessary to provide protection for this one against compaction of snow.

T. occidentalis 'Lutea' grows to some 16′ when mature with an AGR of 6″–8″ and a US of 3′. Another popular name is the George Peabody. This cultivar has been popular for over 100 years. During active growth the tips of the branches are a cream yellow and turn to a golden bronze with the advance of winter.

T. occidentalis 'Rheingold' and 'Ellwangeriana Aurea' and are often mixed up in catalogs. When of a young age, the trees are virtually indistinguishable, since they match in color and foliage type. But 'Rheingold' should be 30″ high and 1′ wide after ten years of growing. 'Ellwangeriana Aurea' will eventually grow to a pyramidal bush 12′ high and some 10′ wide at the base. Both have beautiful foliage that is a pinkish-gold during spring and summer, turning to a burnished bronze for the winter months.

Thuja orientalis (now known as *Platycladus orientalis*) is called the Chinese arborvitae and is not quite as hardy in the Northeast as the native variety. One cultivar is noted.

T. orientalis 'Juniperoides' is only hardy to zone 6 and then needs protection during hard winters. It will grow to some 6′ high in ten years, being some 3′ wide at the base. The notable thing is the foliage: It is gray-green in the summer but turns to a fine blue-purple in the winter. The color of this cultivar is well worth the effort of providing protection and shepherding it along. The problem arises when—after years of effort—the gamble with the weather is lost.

THE HIBA ARBORVITAE

Thujopsis (thuy'-op-sis) is represented by one species, from Japan. In nature it grows to 100'. Here in the American garden it is only hardy to a warm zone 6, no lower than −10°F. The tree form is an almost perfect pyramid and one cultivar is available.

T. dolabrata 'Nana' grows as a bun-shaped bush, forming a loose mound of heavy weeping foliage that is deep green with bronze tints—said to be orange in poor soil—and reaching a height of 2' and a width of 5' in ten years.

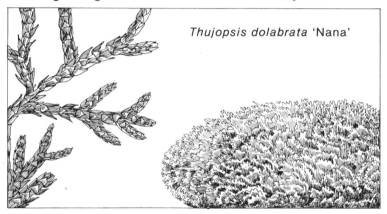

Thujopsis dolabrata 'Nana'

THE HEMLOCKS

My favorite among the evergreens is the hemlock, or *Tsuga canadensis* (sue'-gah). There are ten species, but only *canadensis* and its astounding number of cultivars is of general concern to gardeners.

This eastern hemlock once covered vast acres in the mountains of the New England states and New York, spilling over into Pennsylvania, north through Canada to Nova Scotia, west to Minnesota, and south along the Appalachians to Alabama.

It was first ignored for its timber, since the knots are rock hard, and they quickly dulled old-fashioned equipment. (They will completely devastate the modern home-handyman's power saw.) The floors and walls of our house were framed with hemlock, and a more frustrating wood I've never experienced. After one hundred years it is resilient and tough at the same time.

87

Hemlock's first glory came from the discovery that the bark contained tannin, and a gigantic tanning industry arose around the virgin forests. The shoes of the Civil War troops were made supple with the trees from the Catskill Mountains. Hemlock groves were devastated by greed until the German chemical industry discovered a substitute. By the end of the nineteenth century, all the virgin hemlocks were gone and a vast industry died on its feet.

The trees were monoecious and once reached 100′ in their native groves. Trunks were often 4′ in diameter. Cones

Hemlock branch and cones

are brown and small, and the branches with their ranks of shiny, dark-green needles, bend gracefully toward the ground. All in all, beautiful evergreens, hardy in zone 4.

As witnessed in the woods that surround our house, their soil wants are slight. An acid soil is preferred, and in times of extreme dryness, needles will turn yellow and fall. If this occurs, immediately give them a good soaking and they will soon recover. A mulch is always a good idea.

Finding and growing hemlock seedlings that germinate on the forest floor can lead to a fascinating hobby. These trees will produce a great many variations in color, size of both needle and tree, and the general shape of the tree itself. Since they produce numerous seedlings, the ground that supports a hemlock grove will be covered with plants in various stages of growth. All that is needed is a sharp eye to pick out the few that are different and move them on to a better spot. If left to nature, the mutations will usually die out,

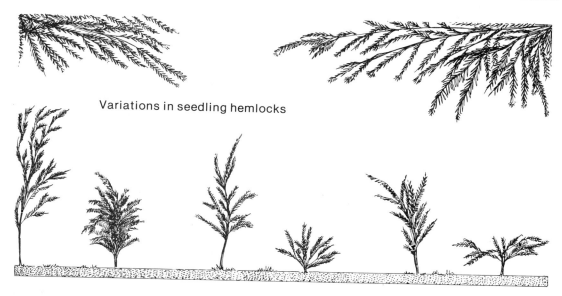

Variations in seedling hemlocks

since they cannot compete with their larger (and more normal) brethren for light and soil nutrients.

Occasionally a dwarf or small variety will suddenly pick up speed and revert to the more original hemlock growth pattern without rhyme or reason.

There are now seventy listed cultivars, and the following listed will grow true to description:

T. canadensis 'Cole' is an absolutely prostrate tree that actually hugs the ground, following contours, and, with a rippled flow, sweeps over and then under the edge of a rock or bank. It prefers some shade and will not do well in hot sun or an exceptional dry position. AGR is 3″ and a plant will cover an area of a 4′ circle in ten years. An older plant resembles a basket starfish with the central branches in evidence but disappearing under needles as it grows to the outer edge. A true rug in the garden, it should be planted in a spot where it's easily visible.

T. canadensis 'Curly' is a small form that has needles that twist and curl about the stem, exposing the silver undersides that contrast with the glossy, dark-green tops. This cultivar should be about 2′ wide and 1½′ high after ten years.

T. canadensis 'Curtis Spreader' is a weeping form that spreads with the branches fanning out on the horizontal, then falling with grace to the earth. It was selected by my neighbor, the Curtis Nurseries of Callicoon, New York, and represents a fine garden form. US is 7′–8′ and UH 6′ after

89

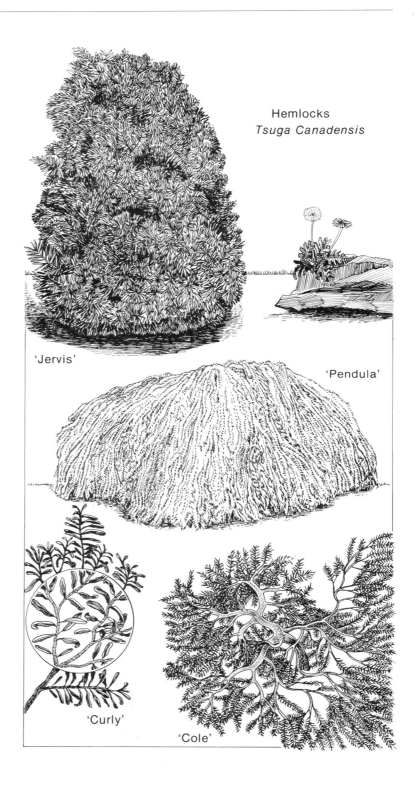

Hemlocks
Tsuga Canadensis

'Jervis'

'Pendula'

'Curly'

'Cole'

twenty-five years. One problem with this and the others; deer find them very good greens during the period of their winter diets.

T. canadensis 'Gentsch White,' or 'Gentsch Variegated,' is a fairly new arrival, discovered on Long Island by Mr. Otto Gentsch, a nurseryman. It has a lacy look with the tips of the branches toned a silvery white. UH is 2', and US is 2'.

T. canadensis 'Hussii' is a very slow-growing hemlock cultivar discovered in the 1930s by Mr. Huss, a park superintendent of Hartford, Connecticut. The main branches will bend at an oblique angle and be short and stubby, reaching a height of 18" after ten years, or perhaps 3' after twenty.

T. canadensis 'Jervis,' or sometimes called 'Nearing,' has yet to grow larger than 30" in any direction after twenty-five years of observation. It forms an irregular pyramid of very compacted growth. This cultivar was discovered in the mid-1960s by Mr. C. G. Nearing in a wooded area some forty miles from my home, just outside Port Jervis, New York.

T. canadensis 'Lewisi' grows as a small pyramid, attaining a height of 1' in ten years.

T. canadensis 'Minuta' brings new meaning to the term *slow-growing*. AGR is two centimeters until a UH of 18" is reached. Since it grows very slowly only from cuttings, the 'Minuta' is the Bently of cultivars in collections of dwarf conifers.

T. canadensis 'Bennett' is also known as 'Bennett's Minima' and grows as a small weeping hemlock with a flattened top some 20" high and 4' wide after twenty years.

T. canadensis 'Pendula' is the weeping hemlock or Sargent's weeping hemlock, discovered near Fishkill, New York, in 1860 by Charles S. Sargent, the first director of the Arnold Arboretum. Here is the Rolls of the hemlock world. The UH is 12'–15', the US 12'–25', and the AGR 2"–3". A mature tree looks for all the world like a shining green mammoth without the tusks, and is best suited as a specimen tree set off by a sweep of lawn.

There is some question as to whether the trees offered today are the same as the original Fishkill discovery, but all share the weeping habit.

TAXACEAE, THE YEW FAMILY

The Yews, or *Taxus* (tax'-us), are a distinct family of evergreens. Though usually thought of as members of the pine family, they differ in having a seed that resembles a berry rather than the typical cone. Plants are either trees or shrubs, and most are dioecious, with male flowers on one and female on the other.

There are eight species, all native to the Northern Hemisphere, but only two are generally found in cultivation: The English yew, *T. baccata,* and the Japanese yew, *T. cuspidata,* plus a number of cultivars developed from a cross of these two, *T. × media.*

Taxus baccata is the English yew, a tree associated with English life for over 1,000 years. Every English churchyard or cemetery is planted with the yew tree; typical estates are decorated with topiary animals clipped and cut from the yew; and the backbone of the English archer in the middle ages was the longbow fashioned from the wood of the yew.

Unfortunately, this picturesque tree is only hardy to the southern parts of zone 6. If left to grow, yews eventually reach a height of 65' and mature over a period 400 to 500 years. In addition, the leaves are poison and must be kept away from livestock and grazing animals.

Soil must be well drained and neutral or slightly alkaline; in England they can grow in a few inches of soil with a base of chalk.

The fruits are red: one seed or nutlet that sits in a small fruitlike cup.

Two cultivars are always available:

T. baccata 'Adpressa' is an extremely slow grower, even for a yew. It resembles a spreading bush or small tree with very short leaves and arose from a seedling yew in England about 1838. After ten years it will reach a height of 5', exhibiting an open habit of growth.

T. baccata 'Aurea' will spread out to 4' in ten years, reaching a height of 2'. In form it resembles the preceding cultivar, but the foliage begins the season as a soft yellow-gold, darkening with age.

Taxus cuspidata, or the Japanese yew, is considered by some botanists to be merely a form of the English species. Whatever its original roots, this is the more valuable of the two in America, since it is hardy south from zone 3 and, if given adequate protection, will grow in parts of zone 2. Authorities also attribute the same poisonous quality to the foliage, but I've noticed over the seasons that wildlife—especially deer—will eat the foliage and continue to do so whenever it's available.

The Japanese yew is also more tolerant of different soil conditions, needing a cool and moist position more than specific pH. The two species can easily be distinguished: The needles of the English species gradually taper toward the tip of the branch, whereas the Japanese needles abruptly taper toward the tip.

Although a few specimens grow to 40'–45', the majority of types are usually below 15', growing more like large shrubs.

T. cuspidata 'Nana' will make a low bush, never taller than 10'. It will grow some 4'–6' wide in ten years and reach a width of 20' in forty years.

The Japanese yew

Taxus × *media* is the result of a cross between the English and Japanese species accomplished by Mr. T. D. Hatfield, superintendent of the Hunnewell Estate in Wellesley, Massachusetts, in 1900. This hybrid combines the qualities of both, is hardy in zone 4, and grows as a pyramid. It is notable for the number of cultivars it has produced, some forty listed in *Hortus III.*

T. × *media* 'Hatfieldii' also originated on the estate that produced the original cross. The form is pyramidal with dense foliage 12' high and 10' across after twenty years of growth.

T. × *media* 'Wardii' is a spreader of a yew. A twenty-year-old plant is only 6' tall and some 20' across, resembling the 'Nana' form of *T. cuspidata.*

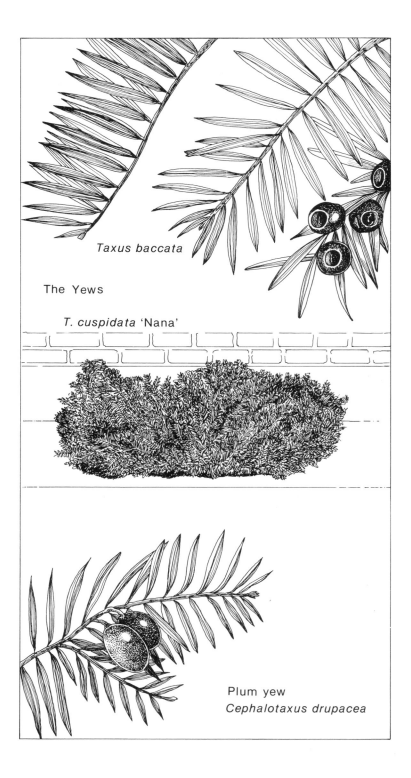

Taxus baccata

The Yews

T. cuspidata 'Nana'

Plum yew
Cephalotaxus drupacea

Cephalotaxus, or the plum yews, are closely allied to the foregoing species but have larger needles and larger fruits. Like yews, they are dioecious, but the flowers appear in the fall rather than spring and fruits are produced the following season. These plants resent hot and dry summers. The typical species is *C. drupacea,* from Japan. It reaches a height of 20′–30′ but rarely grows above 10′ in the garden. It thrives in most ordinary garden soil, but needs protection north of zone 5.

4.

The Broadleaf Evergreens

When entering the world of the broadleaf evergreens, we leave behind the needles of the various pines of the world and their second from the top position in botanical evolution to deal with the true flowering plants, the angiosperms.

The conifers show a great deal of sophistication, but the angiosperms, in addition to the tree species, include herbaceous perennials, annuals, and biennials. Oaks, tulips, and carrots are all angiosperms. In addition to bearing true flowers, they also produce seeds protected by a closed structure, or ovary, unlike the conifers, which lack both flower petals with the accessory parts and produce naked seeds.

But since our main concern is with plants that keep their leaves all year round—no matter what the season or weather—only a small percentage of the flowering plants are covered here. Leaving aside those only suited to the tropics or subtropic regions and overlooking the cactus, the following are of use to the northern gardener:

Boxwoods, brooms, heaths and heathers, *Euonymus,* hollies, laurels, *Leucothoe,* the rhododendrons (including the azaleas), and a number of smaller evergreens usually associated with the wildflowers.

BUXUS, THE BOXWOODS

When the great estates of yesteryear are recalled, one of the first things to come to mind are the vast hedges that surrounded the gates leading to the manor house. When the night was dark, lightning leapt across the sky, and evil was afoot, then Boston Blackie or Charlie Chan would be forced to climb these shrubs to gain surreptitious entrance to the scene of the crime.

We do not suggest that the boxwood of the genus *Buxus* (bux'-us) should surround today's suburban garden, requiring fleets of groundsmen to keep them pruned, but a few of these fine evergreen shrubs planted here or there for a winter accent would be a fine addition.

Cultural requirements are few: Any good garden soil that is well drained; a position that offers some shade (though full sun will do); and an occasional application of fertilizer to the roots after a few years of growth.

These shrubs or small trees are grown for the foliage alone, since the flowers are insignificant.

The boxwoods as a group respond well to clipping and pruning; it's been said that they cannot suffer from too much. Because of this they have been used extensively just for hedges and for topiary. If such is your plan, the best time for clipping—except for a random shear or two—is in the late spring.

Except for a few of the cultivars, these plants do not do well north of the warmer parts of zone 5.

Buxus microphylla is termed the littleleaf box and is only reliably hardy in zone 6. This is a compact shrub, usually growing to a height of 3'. A cultivar called the Korean box (*B. microphylla* var. *koreana*) grows about 2' high and is hardy to zone 4, but the leaves turn an unattractive brownish green in the dead of winter.

Buxus sempervirens is the common box, a native of southern Europe. It was used in gardens of the United States for years, since the colonists brought it with them when emigrating. The species grows to some 20' if left uncut. There are a number of cultivars that produce variations in the leaf, but two are especially interesting.

98

B. sempervirens 'Inglis' forms a dense and dark-green pyramid of growth. Originated in Michigan, it withstands temperatures of − 20°F.

B. sempervirens 'Northern Find' is a cultivar from Canada that forms a rounded bush some 3′ in diameter. It is said to withstand winter temperatures of − 30°F.

Both softwood and hardwood cuttings of boxwood will root without difficulty.

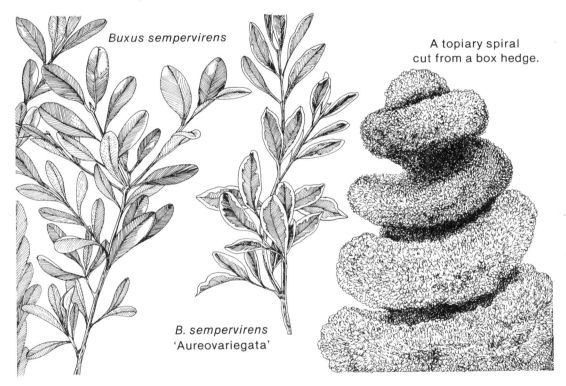

Buxus sempervirens

A topiary spiral cut from a box hedge.

B. sempervirens 'Aureovariegata'

THE *CYTISUS,* OR BROOMS

These have been favorite plants of mine since I first spied them clinging to the sides of rock bluffs in Harriman State Park, thirty miles up the Hudson from New York City. In spring they are covered with pealike blossoms of pink or yellow, and four or five in a group are beyond description. The leaves are small, so small as to be hardly noticed, but the branches are long and whiplike and can best be termed *evergreen,* since they keep their green color all year long.

99

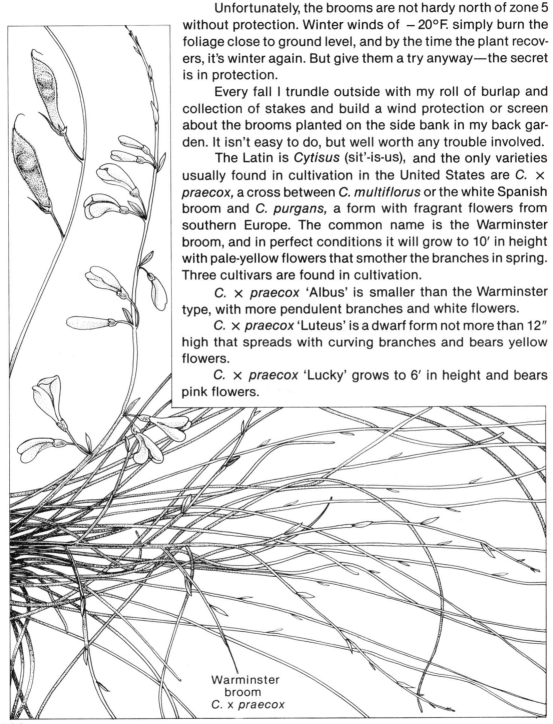

Unfortunately, the brooms are not hardy north of zone 5 without protection. Winter winds of − 20°F. simply burn the foliage close to ground level, and by the time the plant recovers, it's winter again. But give them a try anyway—the secret is in protection.

Every fall I trundle outside with my roll of burlap and collection of stakes and build a wind protection or screen about the brooms planted on the side bank in my back garden. It isn't easy to do, but well worth any trouble involved.

The Latin is *Cytisus* (sit'-is-us), and the only varieties usually found in cultivation in the United States are *C.* × *praecox,* a cross between *C. multiflorus* or the white Spanish broom and *C. purgans,* a form with fragrant flowers from southern Europe. The common name is the Warminster broom, and in perfect conditions it will grow to 10′ in height with pale-yellow flowers that smother the branches in spring. Three cultivars are found in cultivation.

C. × *praecox* 'Albus' is smaller than the Warminster type, with more pendulent branches and white flowers.

C. × *praecox* 'Luteus' is a dwarf form not more than 12″ high that spreads with curving branches and bears yellow flowers.

C. × *praecox* 'Lucky' grows to 6′ in height and bears pink flowers.

Warminster
broom
C. x *praecox*

100

THE HEATHS AND THE HEATHERS

I've grouped these two genera together, since they both belong to the heath family. Both conjure up visions of open moors under brooding Scottish skies and cries of "Heathcliff! Heathcliff!"

The heaths belong to the genus *Erica* (e-rik'-a) and are evergreen shrubs or sometimes trees that share small, evergreen, needlelike leaves. The heathers are *Calluna* (kal-loon'-a). They too are evergreen, but the leaves are shorter, squatter, and overlap each other.

Erica carnea, or the spring heath, is usually only hardy to zone 6 but does survive in zone 5 with adequate protection. The red or white flowers bloom from late February to April, depending on the winter temperatures. They form small mounds of foliage about 1' high and, for all practical purposes, need an acid soil and good drainage. If your soil is heavy or uncut clay, add sharp sand before setting in these plants. They need full sun. Cut them back before they bloom so that any branches killed over the winter are removed rather than taking a chance at cutting off live tissue. If gardening in zone 5 or colder, transplant the heaths and heathers only in spring, thus allowing them plenty of time to settle in.

A fine place to grow these plants is on a bank and/or between plantings of larger evergreen conifers, thus giving added protection from icy winds.

The following are cultivars of *E. carnea:*

E. carnea 'King George' grows 12″ high and blooms from January to May with crimson flowers.

E. carnea 'Springwood White' grows 8″ tall and blooms from January to May with white flowers.

E. carnea 'Springwood Pink' grows 8″ high and produces pink flowers from February to April. A heavy root system helps it spread with ease.

E. carnea 'Winter Beauty' only tops 5″ in height and can bloom in December during a mild winter but usually starts in April. This plant also spreads.

Erica tetralix is one of the hardiest heaths, with gray foliage and rosy flowers blooming from late June to October. This is probably hardy in zone 4.

E. tetralix 'George Fraser' grows from 10″ to 14″ and is

in bloom with rose-pink flowers between late June and October.

The heathers require the same general conditions as the heaths but, as can be seen by their thicker leaf structure, will tolerate colder temperatures. There is only one species, *vulgaris,* and all the *Calluna*s are variations on the one theme. Called lings in England, these shrubby evergreens grow about 18″ high and bloom between late June and November. Never give them rich soil. They, like the heaths, need well-drained but "poor" soil so that growth does not become leggy and blossoms are profuse. The following are cultivars:

C. vulgaris 'Coccinea' grows to 10″ and blooms between August and September with deep crimson flowers.

C. vulgaris 'Gold Haze' grows with golden foliage and produces white flowers on 2′ stems between August and September.

C. vulgaris 'H. E. Beale' grows 24″ high and produces large, double, pink flowers from August to November.

C. vulgaris 'J. H. Hamilton' is a spreader some 10″ high that blooms in August and September with double rose-pink flowers.

C. vulgaris 'Mullion' produces deep-pink flowers starting in late July and remaining through September. Plants grow to 12″ high.

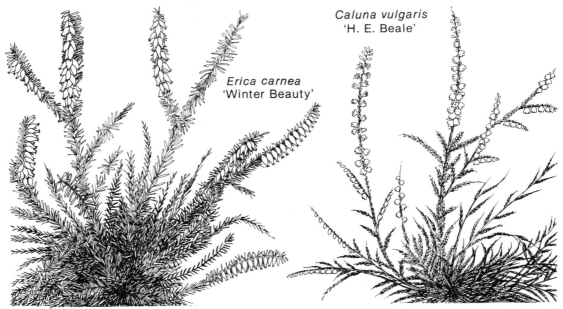

Caluna vulgaris
'H. E. Beale'

Erica carnea
'Winter Beauty'

EUONYMUS

The *Euonymus* (yew-on'-im-us) represent about 170 species of deciduous or evergreen shrubs or small trees, many hardy in the North and requiring no more than ordinary, well-drained soil. They prefer a slightly shady spot and should be well watered as they settle in.

They are susceptible to a scale that encrusts the branches and leaf undersides with a gray or white insect that achieves epidemic proportions. The only solution with heavily infested plants is to shear them to the ground and burn them. If the plague is a light one, any scale-fighting insecticide will do the trick.

Euonymus fortunei, or the wintercreeper, is the hardiest of these plants, and will grow in zone 5. In old books it was called *E. radicans,* and some catalogs still persist in this name. If given a wall, the species will cling to it with tiny rootlets, or will form a small shrub and send trailers out along the ground, covering sizable areas in time. Three cultivars are usually found at nurseries.

E. fortunei 'Minima' is a creeper with tiny, dark-green leaves that clamber over the ground forming a mat 2"–3" high.

E. fortunei 'Argenteo-marginata' either climbs or crawls depending on the location. It has been reliably winter-hardy for me over a five-year period. It rambles along the side of a bank beneath a very large white pine, making a most effective ground cover. The leaves are variegated with green, white, and shades of pink, some having a combination of all three.

E. fortunei 'Colorata' is still called *E. radicans coloratus* in some catalogs. This is a fine vine that will grow under trees and shrubs or clamber about poles and old fenceposts. The leaves are a deep purple that become paler in autumn and winter.

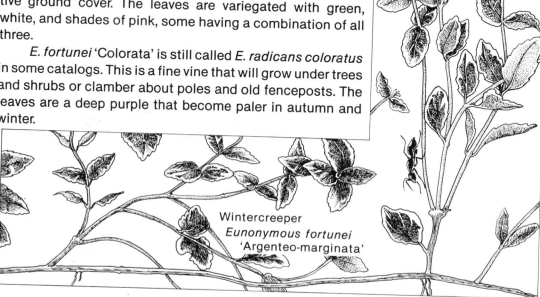

Wintercreeper
Eunonymous fortunei
'Argenteo-marginata'

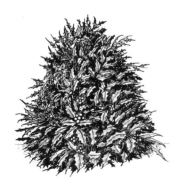

THE *ILEX,* OR HOLLY

With over 400 species listed for the holly family and societies devoted to its culture both in America and England, very little coverage can be given to this most beloved plant in a few pages of text. Suffice it to say that the following only whet your appetite in seeking more about this tree—or shrub—that has been linked with warm feelings of holiday and home for centuries.

Ilex (eye'-lex) was first mentioned in the lore of Christmas during the reign of Henry VI and has been a stock in trade for the florist ever since.

All hollies—except the swampy deciduous species—prefer a fertile and well-rained soil with a sunny disposition. The American holly, *I. opaca,* is one of the few trees that seem to enjoy the rigors of the oceanside climate of Fire Island or the south shore of Long Island in New York State. It grows on sand and gets plenty of rainfall. Not only are the glossy, clipped leaves attractive, but the red berries make the tree a thing of beauty in the garden. In order to have fruit, a male and a female tree must be near each other, since the hollies are monoecious.

Ilex aquifolium, or the English holly, is only hardy to the southern parts of zone 6. It is an exceptionally fine evergreen that can grow to a height of 70' but usually only goes to 30' in the garden and can be clipped or cut to any height desired.

I. aquifolium 'Aureomarginata Ovata' only grows to 10' high and has a lovely yellow margin surrounding the edge of every leaf. It needs a sunny position to keep the color at its best.

I. aquifolium has been crossed with *I. rugosa,* a low-growing form from Japan, to produce *I.* × *Meserveae.* This type grows to a height of only 7' and is said to be quite hardy—when given protection—in zone 5. 'Blue Boy' (nursery names, not mine) is the male and 'Blue Princess' is the female. Remember to plant at least one of each for berries.

Ilex opaca is the American holly, growing to about 50'. According to *Hortus III,* there are over one thousand named cultivars of this species listed in the *International Checklist of Cultivated Ilex;* the mind boggles. The difference between the American and English is that the American bears fruit on the current year's growth and the leaves do not have a high, shiny gloss.

Since the holly has been on the human scene for so many years, some superstitions have followed its planting. William Dallimore's charming book *Holly, Yew, and Box* offers the following prescription for a maiden to find a husband: she "must place three pails of water on her bedroom floor, then pin three leaves of green Holly to her nightdress over her heart, and retire to bed. She will be aroused from her first sleep by three terrible yells, followed by three horse laughs, after which the form of her future husband will appear. If he is deeply attached to her, he will change the position of the water pails; if not, he will glide from the room without touching them."

The address of the Holly Society of America is listed in Chapter 5.

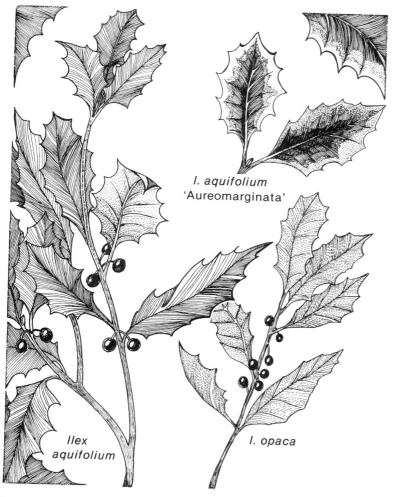

I. aquifolium
'Aureomarginata'

Ilex aquifolium

I. opaca

THE *KALMIA,* OR LAURELS

The *Kalmia* (kal'-mia) genus comprises evergreen members of the heath family. They only grow in acid soils and, because of their thin and wiry root systems, require a moist, somewhat shady location. Called the mountain laurel, it has white or rose-colored flowers that carpet the mountains of the East every year in early June. So profuse are the blossoms in years that follow mild winters that hills seem to be covered with pink snow.

The lanceolate leaf has an undersurface of a light green; it looks like a cross between the rhododendron and the azalea leaf.

Since these plants must have an acid soil, it is recommended that at least a bushel of peat and leaf mold (3/4 to 1/4) be mixed in the site soil, then moistened well and allowed to settle for a few days before planting. Make sure the peat is moist—dry peat is impossible to mix and water will roll right off.

K. latifolia is the true mountain laurel and quite hardy just outside my door, where winter temperatures have been known to plunge to − 25°F. Over a period of years the plants will form a small grove, since they spread by suckers. Height rarely goes above 10′, though established groves can soar to 20′ or more. Color varies between almost white to a deep, dark rose, and years of satisfaction await the gardener who wishes to establish a few of the available cultivars. 'Rubra' is the red-flowered form and 'Alba' the white.

Mountain laurel
Kalmia latifolia

Sheep laurel
K. angustifolia

K. angustifolia is also known as sheep laurel or lambkill, since it is reputed to be poisonous to livestock. Growing no higher than 3′, sheep laurel is hardier than mountain laurel, doing well in zone 3. Though not as attractive as the other type, it is a little less choosy about growing conditions, and the flowers, though not as large as the mountain laurel's, are just as beautiful.

K. polifolia, or the bog laurel, makes an excellent ground cover in boggy situations. It grows to about 2′ tall and is hardy to zone 2.

LEUCOTHOE

Leucothoe (lew-ko'-tho-ee), or mountain andromeda, is an underrated evergreen shrub that belongs to the heath family. Like others of the group, it requires an acid soil and tolerates some shade. Though the foliage is attractive in itself, the plants also bear small, bell-shaped flowers of white to blue, quite similar to blueberry blossoms.

L. davisiae, or the sierra laurel, grows to about 5' high and is hardy to zone 6. The leaves are lustrous and dark green and the waxy white flowers are borne above the foliage.

L. fontanesiana, or doghobble, is hardy to zone 5 and does well in my backyard—but unfortunately animals love the leaves in the dead of winter and I often forget to cage it. This shrub will grow to 6' tall, and the white flowers hang in racemes under the stems. The leaves turn a bronzy red in fall and most last through the winter. When a plant gets too old, it becomes straggly-looking and stems longer than 3' in length look best when cut off at ground level and allowed to grow again.

L. fontanesiana 'Rainbow' grows to about 5' in height and the leaves are irregularily marked with creamy yellow. New growth is tinged with pink.

L. fontanesiana 'Nana' will only reach a height of 2' but

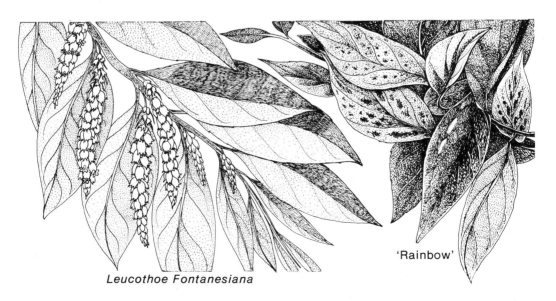

Leucothoe Fontanesiana

'Rainbow'

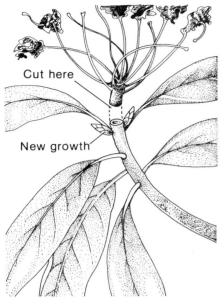

Cut here

New growth

Removing spent blossoms

will spread over an area of 5'–6' after some twenty-five years of growth.

L. 'Scarletta' is a new variety, the result of a cross between L. axillaris, a shrub from the Southeast, and L. fontanesiana. It is exceptionally hardy, growing no taller than 20', and is said to require no pruning. The new growth is bright red and remains so until the leaves turn to a burgundy color for winter.

THE *RHODODENDRONS*

When entering the world of the rhododendrons, one must be prepared for a world complete unto itself. Many gardeners have started with one or two plants and wound up abandoning all else and making these plants the object of a lifelong pursuit.

The genus *Rhododendron* (rho-do-den'-dron) represents some 800 species of evergreen and deciduous shrubs—and a few trees—chiefly found in the Northern Hemisphere, especially in the Himalayas.

Those horticulturists who deal with these magnificent plants have divided them into various sections and categories based on botanical differences. But for most purposes it is only necessary to know that there are two major divisions in the group: rhododendrons and azaleas. Both belong to the same genus, but azaleas are usually deciduous and have flowers shaped like funnels, whereas rhododendrons are usually evergreen and have bell-shaped flowers.

Cultural requirements for each are the same: a well-drained acidic soil composed of leaf mold combined with peat and sand; heavy clay and alkaline soils are slow death to the whole group.

They also prefer a location that protects them from both the continuous heat of a summer sun and harsh winds in summer or winter. Their root systems are shallow and thinly branched so that both plants need a soil that remains continually moist.

Nurseries that specialize in growing and selling rhododendron species and hybrids have a careful habit of listing the climate requirements: Though some species are hardy in the bitter winter winds of the Northeast—especially when

108

American rhododendron
Rhododendron maximum

planted in protected spots—most prefer winter temperatures above 0°F. The following plants are but a sample of the
endless varieties now available to the gardener.

Generally rhododendrons should be planted out in the
early spring; the plants are waking from winter slumber and
ready to shoot into growth and flowering. This schedule is
especially important in the North, since it gives plants adequate time for settling in before the coming winter.

Planting preparations are much the same as for other
evergreens: The hole must be large enough for the roots to
spread out. Set the root ball so that the base of the trunk is on
a level with the soil surface and fill the hole with a mixture of
peat and sand, three parts to one. Firm the soil, tamping it
down with fervor. Keep the soil moist and follow it up with a
careful watering schedule for the remainder of the growing
season.

109

The following rhododendrons are all hybrids between species, species and other hybrids, or hybrids crossed with hybrids. For simplification only the cultivar names are given.

R. 'Anah Kruschke' is hardy in zone 5, growing to a height of 6' and blooming in mid-May with red-purple flowers. This particular cultivar will withstand more sun than most others.

R. 'Pink Pearl' has been in cultivation since the late 1800s and won an Award of Merit from the Royal Horticultural Society in 1897. The UH is 6', and the flowers are a deep pink in bud and a paler pink when they open. It is said to be one of the most popular cultivars ever developed. It blooms in May.

R. 'Ramapo' is hardy in zone 5 and blooms in early May with pale violet flowers on a bush some 2' high. It too will take more sun than average and is especially suited for the rock garden or small landscape.

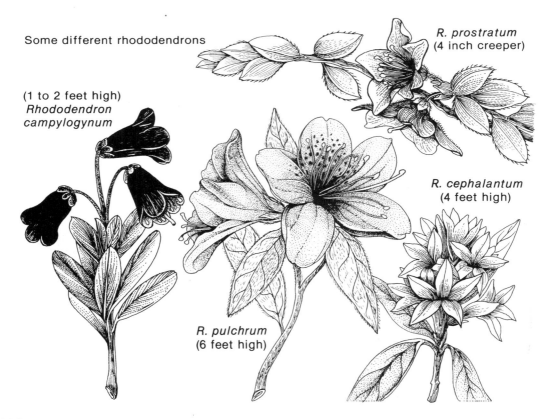

Some different rhododendrons

R. prostratum
(4 inch creeper)

(1 to 2 feet high)
Rhododendron
campylogynum

R. cephalantum
(4 feet high)

R. pulchrum
(6 feet high)

R. 'Unique' grows to 4' in height and is hardy in zone 6. Flowers appear in early May, opening with a bright pink but turning to a beautiful creamy white.

R. 'Edward Dunn' grows to 5' tall and is only hardy to zone 7. Its special interest lies in its blooming so late in the season. The yellow-orange flowers appear in late June.

In addition to the hybrids, there are the following *Rhododendron* species: *R. luteum* has a fragrant yellow flower adorning a small bush that grows some 4' high. It blooms in early May and is hardy in zone 5.

R. maximum, or the great laurel, is the native American rhododendron from the mountains of Pennsylvania and southern New York south to the Carolinas. It grows to 15' in height, but some older groves have specimens of great age that may reach to a height of 30'. The flowers produce a honey reputed to be poisonous, indeed fatal to ingest. This plant and its cultivars are hardy to zone 4.

Azaleas are for the most part deciduous, but the following evergreens are hardy to zone 6 and the southern parts of zone 5. In my area of the mountains only one evergreen azalea is remotely hardy—a cultivar from the Curtis nurseries, and even that cannot suffer through too many bitter winters.

R. 'Anchorite' has blossoms of rose pink on bushes 4' in height. Blooming is in late April and early May.

R. 'Mother's Day' has magnificent blossoms of rose red that appear in early May on bushes 2'–3' high.

R. 'Treasure' grows 4'–5' high and bears flowers of white that are unusually large and appear in early spring.

R. 'Hino Crimson' is hardy in zone 5. Its dark-green foliage is topped with rose-pink flowers on a bush some 3' high and 3' wide after ten years of growth. This is an especially fine cultivar and a good specimen will be literally covered with blossoms.

SOME SMALLER EVERGREENS

The following plants are all evergreens, and all have successfully managed to make it through true northern winters and still flower the following spring. Of small habit, most are at their best in a wild garden or some protected area that gives ample sun in March and April but offers shade from the noon suns of July and August.

Arctostaphylos, or Bearberry

Arctostaphylos (ark-to-staff'-il-oss) is another member of the popular heath family, but this small ground cover is completely hardy as far north as zone 2. Called bearberry or kinikinick, the entire name is *A. uva-ursi.* It's a native across the country from coast to coast and is valued both for the fine foliage—turning a rich bronze in fall—and the red berries that follow the small bell-shaped flowers. The only requirement is that soil be well drained.

Bears are said to like the flowers and the second common name *kinikinick,* refers to an Indian use of the leaves for tobacco.

Asarum, or Wild Ginger

Asarum shuttleworthi, or wild ginger, is a small plant that is perfect for a ground cover. It prefers an acid soil and full shade after the heat of a summer sun builds up. The heart-

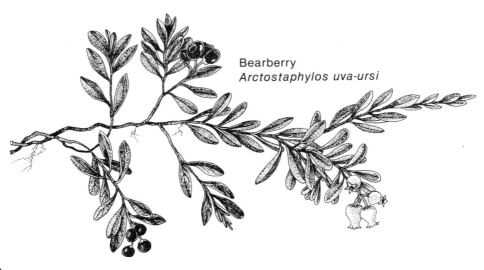

Bearberry
Arctostaphylos uva-ursi

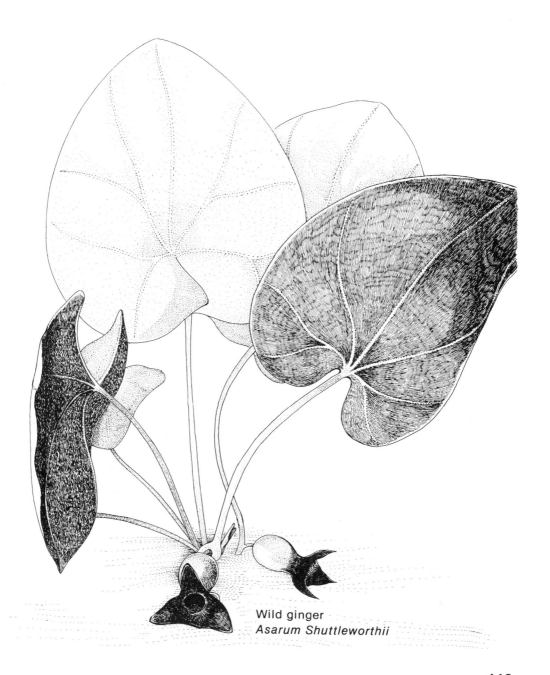

Wild ginger
Asarum Shuttleworthii

shaped leaves grow only a few inches high and the flowers resemble "little brown jugs" that lie directly on the ground, each one attached to the base of a leaf. They need some humus in the soil and suffer during periods of long drought. Hardy in zone 6.

A. europaeum is the European wild ginger, hardy to zone 5. The leaves grow 2'–3″ wide on 5″ stalks, and the flowers are greenish purple.

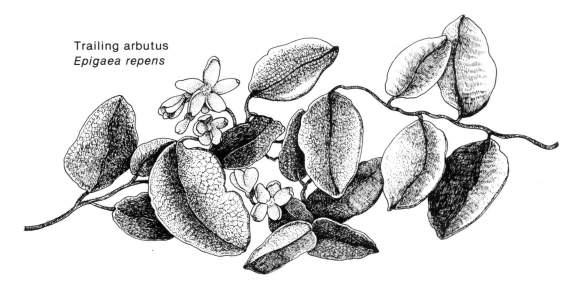

Trailing arbutus
Epigaea repens

Epigaea, or Trailing Arbutus

Epigaea (ep-i-jee'-a) *repens* is the trailing arbutus and one of the most beloved and enamored wildflower ever grown. The white to pink flowers appear in Late April to early May and are very fragrant. The 3″-long leaves lie flat upon the ground and form an evergreen mat. Plants require an extremely acid soil, extra moisture during dry spells, and a winter mulch, pine needles doing the job nicely. Don't dig them up from woodlands; they rarely transplant well, and most states now protect them with penalty if the transplanter is caught—and anyone stealing on this level deserves to be. They can be readily purchased by mail.

Galax, or Wandflower

Galax (gay'-lax) *rotundifolia,* or the wandflower, bears shiny, evergreen leaves of heart-shaped motif that turn to a bronzy-

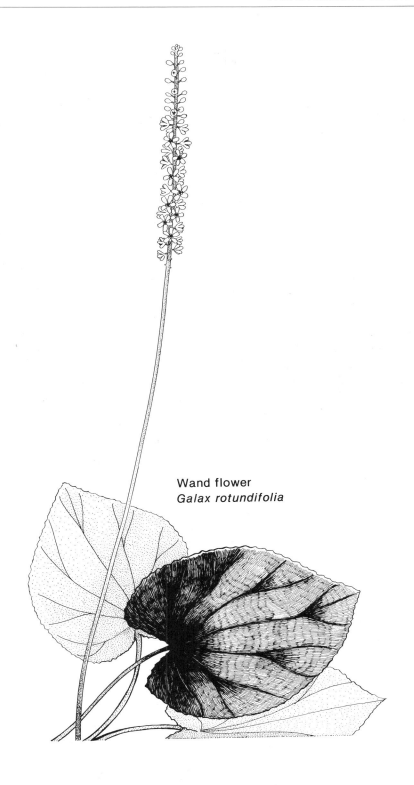

Wand flower
Galax rotundifolia

red in winter. They are hardy in zone 6 and in zone 5 with a winter mulch. They like acid and moist soil in the shade. In spring they bear a 6″–12″ stalk of small, white flowers, each of which has five petals. They make an efficient ground cover, since their creeping rootstocks quickly spread about. The old name, still found, is *G. aphylla.*

Gaultheria, or Wintergreen

Gaultheria (gawl-thee'-ria) is still another member of the heath family. It is the source of commercial wintergreen. The species name is *procumbens,* referring to its growth habit of staying close to the ground. The drooping, waxy, bell-like flowers are usually hidden by the shiny-green foliage, but the large red berries that appear in the fall are a familiar sight to anyone who takes autumn walks in the woods. Soil should be acid, moist, and lightly shaded, and if happy in its situation, wintergreen will form a fine ground cover.

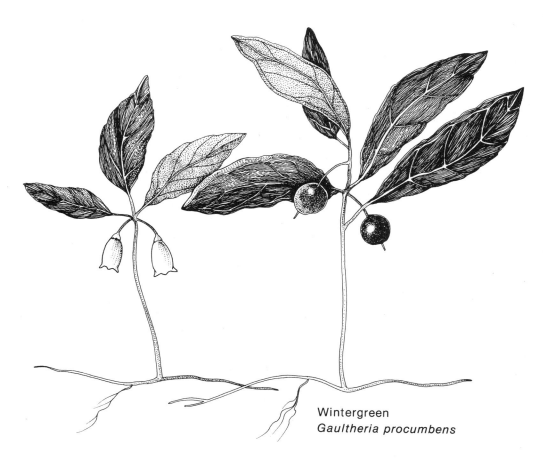

Wintergreen
Gaultheria procumbens

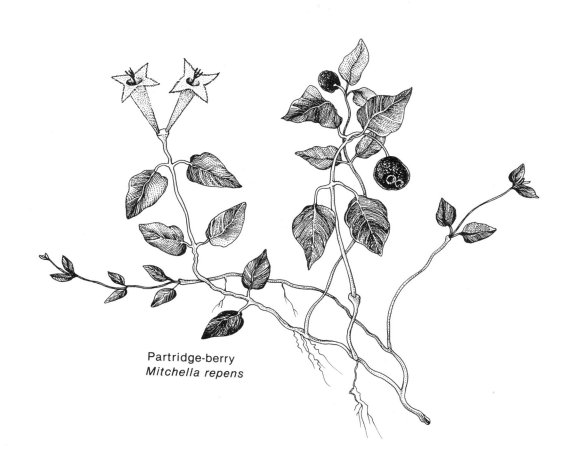

Partridge-berry
Mitchella repens

Mitchella, or Partridge-Berry

Mitchella (mich-ell'-a) *repens* is a common inhabitant of the woods of eastern North America and is usually familiar to city dwellers as the plant with the red berries that grows in florist's terrariums. In the garden it will make an effective ground cover if given a moist, acid soil, with some humus and a shady spot. Two pink flowers are borne on a single stalk in the early spring. By late fall the two flowers fuse to form one scarlet berry that remains on the plant until eaten by wildlife.

117

Paxistima

Paxistima (pax-iss'-tima) *canbyi* is a charming evergreen native of North America. It needs an acid soil and, though preferring a bit of shade, will grow in the full sun up North if not kept too dry. The leaves are less than an inch long and turn a beautiful bronze color in the fall. The flowers are tiny and the fruit a small capsule that is easily missed. These plants are grown in clumps to form a charming but small hedge.

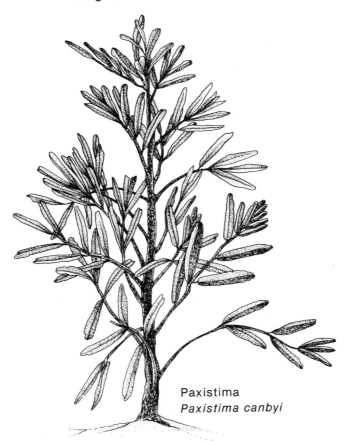

Paxistima
Paxistima canbyi

Shortia, **or Onconee-Bells**

Shortia (short'-ia) *galacifolia* has shiny, evergreen leaves that turn to red or bronze in the fall, creeping low to the ground. It must have a moist but well-drained spot with very acid soil, in the shade. No lime allowed—even water that passes over or through an old foundation that once had cement will prevent the plant from ever doing well. In zone 4 it needs a winter mulch of leaves or pine needles. The flowers must be seen to

Oconee-Bells
Shortia galacifolia

be appreciated; there is not another quite as beautiful in this class of ground cover. The only other members of the genus are found in Japan. This species originally grew only in North and South Carolina.

Vinca, **or Periwinkle**

Vinca (vin'-ka) *minor,* or Periwinkle, is an evergreen ground cover that does well in either sun or shade and is quite happy as far north as zone 4. It was originally brought over from Europe with the colonists but has since escaped from cultivation and is found in fields and old lots and especially in old cemeteries. It covers ground in all but the worst of soils, since the stems root whenever a node touches the ground.

119

The flowers are, of course, periwinkle blue. Three cultivars are available.

V. minor 'Alba' bears white flowers.

V. minor 'Bowles Variety' has larger-than-type flowers of a light blue.

V. minor 'Variegata' has blue flowers as the type, but the leaves are streaked with a rich yellow tone.

Periwinkle
Vinca minor

5.

Buying by Mail and Sources of Supply

Usually a list of suppliers is found at the back of the book and printed in very small type. Hardly the thing to do with the most important link in the gardener's chain. For unless you are lucky enough to live close to a major nursery in the United States or Canada and can drive directly to a supplier for plants, you must rely on mail order.

You need not fear the prospect of ordering plants by mail. The level of honesty of the nurseries of America is of the highest order and except for a few who merchandise year-round tomato vines that also bear potatos and like vegetable monstrosities, they are all to be trusted. They love plants and are dedicated to keeping their consumers happy, for that's the only way to insure a growing business.*

*This following remark is in a footnote, since it must be said but should not interrupt the flow of the list of suppliers. It concerns the U.S. mail. Nobody uses the mails to ship plants at this writing. Someday it could happen again but not until a greater degree of responsibility is evidenced by the postal authorities. If all the members of this so-called business created by Congress to make a profit—with what is a constitutional right—were gardeners or cared about plants, shipments would go forth with dispatch. Until then, the vast majority of nurseries use independent carriers, chiefly United Parcel Service.

I have not given prices for catalogs. This, in inflationary times would be unfair to the nursery. Within two years, the price asked to cover expenses today might merely cover the cost of return postage tomorrow. When in doubt, just drop a card to those nurseries that interest you; they will reply.

The Bovee's Nursery
1737 S.W. Coronado Street
Portland, Oregon 97219

A large selection of small and dwarf conifers, shrubs, azaleas, and rhododendrons.

Brimfield Gardens Nursery
3109 Main Street
Rocky Hill, Connecticut 06067

An extensive selection of small evergreens.

Chrome Run Nursery
350 Howarth Road
Media, Pennsylvania 19063

An exceptional collection of small evergreens. Unfortunately, they do not ship.

The Cummins' Garden
22 Robertsville Road
Marlboro, New Jersey 07746

Rhododendrons and azaleas and a generous selection of popular evergreens.

Dilatush Nursery
780 Route 130
Robbinsville, New Jersey, 08691

No shipping, but the collections are fine and worth the trip if you're in the Northeast.

Forestfarm
990 Tetherow Road
Williams, Oregon 97544

Unusual collection of native evergreens.

BUYING BY MAIL AND SOURCES OF SUPPLY

Girard Nurseries
P.O. Box 428
Geneva, Ohio 44041

Evergreen seedlings, many yews, rhododendrons, azaleas, and a good selection of conifers.

Greer Gardens
1280 Goodpasture Island Road
Eugene, Oregon 97401

Large and colorful catalog covering almost everything, particularly rhododendrons.

Hortica Gardens
P.O. Box 308
Placerville, California 95667

Many azaleas and a large selection of small evergreens.

Lamb Nurseries
E. 101 Sharp Avenue
Spokane, Washington 99202

Good selection of rock plants and baby evergreens.

Mellingers
2310 W. South Range Road
North Lima, Ohio 44452

Large selection of young small evergreens.

Miniature Gardens
P.O. Box 757
Stony Plain, Alberta
TOE 2GO Canada

Very unusual small evergreens for the rock garden.

Musser Forests, Inc.
Indiana, Pennsylvania 15701

Large selection of conifers and broadleaf evergreens.

E. B. Nauman
324 Avalon Drive
Rochester, New York 14618

Rhododendrons, azaleas, and other broadleaf evergreens.

123

Oliver Nurseries, Inc.
1159 Bronson Road
Fairfield, Connecticut 06430

Fine catalog. No shipping, but if you are close enough to drive it is well worth the trip.

Rakestraws
G-3094 S. Term Street
Burton, Michigan 48529

Dwarf conifers for the rock garden.

Rice Creek Gardens
1315 66th Avenue, N.E.
Minneapolis, Minnesota 55432

Dwarf conifers for the rock garden.

The Rock Garden
RFD 2
Litchfield, Maine 04350

Extensive list of dwarf and small conifers plus rhododendrons.

Siskiyou Rare Plant Nursery
2825 Cummings Road
Medford, Oregon 97501

Rare evergreens for the rock garden.

Joel W. Spingarn
1535 Forest Avenue
Baldwin, New York 11510

One of the most extensive collections of small evergreens in existence.

Washington Evergreen Nursery
P.O. Box 125
South Salem, New York 10590

Another outstanding collection of small evergreens.

Wayside Gardens
Hodges, South Carolina 29695

Evergreens—both conifers and rhododendrons.

White Flower Farm
Litchfield, Connecticut 06759

Fine selection of small evergreens, including large selection of heaths and heathers.

Sherway Garden Centers
Etobicoke, Ontario M9C 1A1

Nine garden centers in Canada: seven in Ontario and two in Quebec.

J. C. Bakker Nurseries
RR #3, 3rd St. South
St. Catherines, Ontario, L2R 6P9

John Connon Nusery
Box 200
Waterdown, Ontario L0R 2H0

Catalog free in Canada

McConnell's Nursery, Inc.
RR #1
Port Burwell, Ontario N0J 1T0

Catalog free in Canada

SOCIETIES TO JOIN

The following societies are active in the United States or England and all help the member expand his garden horizons by trading information and enlarging collections by trading plants or growing from seeds.

Alpine Garden Society
Lye End Link, St. John's
Woking GU21 1SW
Surrey, England

American Boxwood Society
P.O. Box 85
Boyce, Virginia 22620

American Horticultural Society
7931 East Boulevard Drive
Alexandria, Virginia 22308

American Rhododendron Society
Mrs. Robert Berry
617 Fairway Drive
Aberdeen, Washington 98520

American Rock Garden Society
Donald Peach
P.O. Box 183
Hales Corners, Wisconsin 53130

Holly Society of America
Bluett C. Green, Jr.
407 Fountain Green Road
Bel Air, Maryland 21014

Scottish Rock Garden Club
R. H. D. Orr, C. A.
70 High Street, Haddington
East Lothian, Scotland

Bibliography

Bailey, L. H. *The Cultivated Conifers in North America.* New York: The Macmillan Company, 1933.

Now long out of print, this book is often found in old bookstores or search services. Though some nomenclatures are out of date, it is still a valuable sourcebook on the evergreen conifers in America.

Bartrum, Donald. *Evergreens for Your Garden.* London: John Gifford Ltd. (125 Charing Cross Road, London, WC 2), 1967.

Although written for the English gardener and geared for climates of above 10°F. at the coldest, this book contains much evergreen information.

Bawden, H. E. *Dwarf Shrubs.* Woking, Surrey, England: The Alpine Garden Society (Lye End Link, St. Johns, Woking, Surrey, GU21 1SW), 1980.

Written for the rock gardener in general; a number of dwarf evergreens are covered with an emphasis on container and trough gardening.

Carr, David. *Conifers.* London: B. T. Batsford, Ltd. (4 Fitzhardinge Street, London W1H 0AH), 1979.

A fine book on conifers for the garden but lacking good illustrations.

Chittenden, Fred J., ed. *Dictionary of Gardening of the Royal Horticultural Society.* Oxford: The Clarendon Press, 1974.

One of the best encyclopedic approaches to gardening ever published. A major investment but valuable for all gardening whether conifers or hot-house plants.

Dallimore, William. *Holly, Yew, and Box.* Little Compton, R.I.: Theophrastus (Garland STPM Press, 545 Madison Avenue, New York, N.Y. 10022), 1977.

One of the fine Theophrastus publications of old but reliable books; the original first appearing in 1908.

Gault, S. M., and Kalmbacher, George. *The Color Dictionary of Shrubs.* New York: Crown Publishers, 1976.

Fine color photos of rhododendrons, azaleas, and many conifers. Published with the collaboration of the Royal Horticultural Society. Effort has been made to help the American gardener.

Harrison, Charles R. *Ornamental Conifers.* New York: Hafner Press, 1975.

An absolutely top-notch book dealing with many of the best ornamental conifers, with page after page of fine color photos.

Hilliers and Sons. *Hillier's Manual of Trees and Shrubs.* Newton Abbot, England: David & Charles, 1974.

A concise listing of all the known—and available—cultivars of most evergreens. Perhaps not to own but fine to consult.

Hornibrook, Murray. *Dwarf and Slow-growing Conifers.* Little Compton, R.I.: Theophrastus, 1973.

Another classic in the field of ornamental conifers. If you are a serious grower, this is a must for the library.

Hortus III. New York: The Macmillan Company, 1976.

A most valuable reference work, especially for the correct botanical names. Climate zones are usually on the conservative side and often open to some experiment.

Huxley, Anthony, ed. *Evergreen Garden Trees and Shrubs.* New York: The Macmillan Company, 1973.

One of Macmillan's valuable pocket series but written in England.

Mathews, F. Schuyler. *Field Book of American Trees and Shrubs*. New York: G. P. Putnam's Sons, 1915.

Reprinted over the years and the best available for identifying trees and shrubs in the wild. Never condescending in tone, this book assumes that any reader will have a modicum of intelligence.

Petrides, George A. *A Field Guide to Trees and Shrubs*. Boston: Houghton Mifflin Company, 1972.

One of the Peterson Field Guide Series with color (green) added to the illustrations and very straightforward in its approach to identification, but not as good or as complete as Mr. Mathews's book.

Proudley, Brian and Valerie. *Garden Conifers in Color*. Poole, Dorset, England: Blandford Press, 1976.

A fine little book with excellent color photographs dealing with most of the more common garden conifers.

Taylor, Norman. *The Guide to Garden Shrubs and Trees*. New York: Bonanza Books (Crown Publishers), 1965.

Lists many of the more common evergreen trees and shrubs for the large and small garden. Zone designations are confusing, since zone 1 is 0°F. or below using average minimum temperatures for the coldest month; this would be zone 6 in most other reference books.

Welch, Humphrey J. *Manual of Dwarf Conifers*. New York: Theophrastus (Garland STPM Press, 545 Madison Avenue, New York, N.Y. 10022), 1979.

Another fine book by Theophrastus and a major contribution to the literature on dwarf conifers.

Wyman, Donald. *Dwarf Shrubs*. New York: The Macmillan Company, 1975.

Covers many of the small evergreens, both conifers and flowering plants.

Wyman's Gardening Encyclopedia. New York: The Macmillan Company, 1971.

A fine reference book and one of the best to have in the library. Easy to use and easy to read, covering many facts on small evergreens among many pages covering other subjects devoted to gardening in general.

Index

130

131